AF715123

Mastering Google Cloud Platform: Navigating the Clouds

Kameron Hussain and Frahaan Hussain

Published by Sonar Publishing, 2024.

While every precaution has been taken in the preparation of this book, the publisher assumes no responsibility for errors or omissions, or for damages resulting from the use of the information contained herein.

MASTERING GOOGLE CLOUD PLATFORM: NAVIGATING THE CLOUDS

First edition. March 9, 2024.

Copyright © 2024 Kameron Hussain and Frahaan Hussain.

ISBN: 979-8224782536

Written by Kameron Hussain and Frahaan Hussain.

Table of Contents

containerized applications with ease. GKE offers features such as automatic scaling, automatic node upgrades, and node auto-repair to ensure the availability and reliability of your container workloads.

2. Horizontal Pod Autoscaling (HPA)**: In Kubernetes, you can configure Horizontal Pod Autoscaling (HPA) to automatically adjust the number of pod replicas based on resource utilization metrics such as CPU or memory usage. GKE supports HPA, allowing your application to scale dynamically in response to changing workloads.

3. Stackdriver Kubernetes Monitoring**: Stackdriver is a GCP service that provides comprehensive monitoring and logging for containerized applications. It allows you to gain insights into the performance and health of your containers, clusters, and workloads. You can set up alerts, create custom dashboards, and troubleshoot issues effectively.

4. Cloud Logging and Cloud Monitoring**: GCP offers Cloud Logging and Cloud Monitoring, which are integrated with GKE. Cloud Logging allows you to collect, view, and analyze logs generated by your containers and applications. Cloud Monitoring enables you to set up custom metrics, create alerts, and monitor the performance of your containerized workloads.

5. Node Pools**: GKE allows you to create multiple node pools within a cluster, each with its own configuration and characteristics. Node pools can be used to optimize resource allocation for different workloads. For example, you can create a node pool with high CPU resources for

CPU-intensive tasks and another with high memory resources for memory-intensive tasks.

6. Auto-Scaling**: GKE supports automatic node scaling based on the utilization of node resources. You can configure auto-scaling policies to ensure that your cluster adapts to varying workloads, adding or removing nodes as needed.

7. Custom Metrics**: GKE allows you to define custom metrics and thresholds for auto-scaling your workloads. This gives you the flexibility to scale based on application-specific metrics and requirements.

8. Cluster Management**: GCP provides various tools and features for managing clusters efficiently. You can upgrade the Kubernetes version of your clusters, enable automatic security patching, and perform rolling updates to keep your clusters up to date and secure.

Chapter 6: Developing and Deploying Applications

6.1 Building Applications in the Cloud

Cloud-Native Application Development

Choosing the Right Compute Service

Continuous Integration and Continuous Deployment (CI/CD)

Serverless Solutions

Monitoring and Logging

6.2 Choosing the Right Computing Service for Your Application

1. Rightsizing Resources

2. Auto-scaling

3. Resource Cleanup

4. Use Committed Use Contracts

5. Use Sustained Use Discounts

6. Leverage Preemptible VMs

7. Optimize Storage

8. Monitor and Set Alerts

9. Budgeting and Cost Control

10. Use Google Cloud's Cost Management Tools

11. Review and Optimize Licensing

12. Evaluate Service Usage

13. Explore Complementary Services

14. Cost Optimization Best Practices

Section 11.5: Case Studies: Scalable Architectures in GCP

1. Spotify: Scaling Music Streaming

2. Snapchat: Managing User Growth

3. Niantic: Hosting Augmented Reality Games

4. Zynga: Supporting Online Games

5. Twitter: Analyzing Real-Time Data

6. Data Transformation with Dataflow

7. Analyze Data with BigQuery

8. Visualize Data with Data Studio and Looker

9. Alerting and Monitoring

10. Device Management and Updates

11. Scalability and Security

12. Cost Optimization

Section 13.4: Analyzing IoT Data in the Cloud

1. Data Preprocessing

2. Real-Time Data Streaming

3. Data Storage

4. Data Analysis Tools

5. Machine Learning and AI

6. Real-Time Monitoring and Alerts

7. Data Security and Compliance

8. Scalability and Performance

9. Cost Optimization

10. Iterative Analysis and Improvement

Section 13.5: Case Studies: IoT Implementations Using GCP

1. Smart Manufacturing

Automation Tools in Google Cloud

Infrastructure as Code (IaC) Best Practices

Section 16.5: Best Practices for Cloud Automation

1. Define Clear Objectives: Before implementing automation, clearly define your objectives and what you want to achieve. Determine the key tasks or processes that would benefit from automation.

2. Start Small: If you're new to automation, start with small, well-defined tasks. As you gain experience and confidence, gradually expand automation to more complex processes.

3. Use Infrastructure as Code (IaC): Implement IaC principles using tools like Google Deployment Manager or Terraform. This allows you to version control your infrastructure, manage it as code, and easily replicate environments.

4. Apply the Principle of Least Privilege: When configuring automation scripts and tools, follow the principle of least privilege (POLP). Ensure that automation processes only have the necessary permissions to perform their tasks, reducing security risks.

5. Regularly Review and Update: Automation scripts and configurations should be regularly reviewed and updated. As your infrastructure evolves, your automation should adapt accordingly.

6. Documentation and Comments: Document your automation scripts and configurations thoroughly. Include comments to explain complex or critical sections. This helps other team members understand and troubleshoot.

7. Testing and Validation: Implement automated testing for your automation code. Test deployments, configurations, and workflows to catch errors before they affect production environments.

8. Backup and Recovery: Consider automated backup and recovery processes. Regularly back up critical data and configurations, and ensure that recovery processes are tested and reliable.

9. Monitor Automation: Use monitoring and alerting tools to keep an eye on your automation processes. Set up alerts for failures or unexpected behavior so that you can respond promptly.

10. Scalability and Performance: Design automation with scalability in mind. Ensure that your automation can handle increased workloads as your infrastructure grows.

11. Security Automation: Automate security checks and compliance audits. This includes scanning for vulnerabilities, ensuring proper access controls, and maintaining encryption standards.

12. Lifecycle Management: Implement automation for resource lifecycle management. Automatically decommission resources that are no longer needed to optimize costs.

13. Collaboration: Encourage collaboration among team members working on automation. Use version control systems and collaboration platforms to share and manage code.

14. Disaster Recovery Testing: Regularly test your disaster recovery processes and automation to ensure they work as expected during critical situations.

15. Keep Abreast of Updates: Stay informed about updates and changes in the cloud environment, as they may impact your automation. Ensure that your scripts and configurations are up to date.

16. Training and Skill Development: Invest in training and skill development for your team members involved in automation. Staying current with best practices and new tools is essential.

17. Cost Optimization: Use automation to monitor and optimize costs. Implement policies that automatically scale resources based on demand or shut down idle resources.

18. Review and Audit Logs: Enable and regularly review logs generated by your automation processes. This helps in troubleshooting issues and maintaining transparency.

19. Compliance and Governance: Implement automation to enforce compliance policies and governance standards across your cloud environment.

20. Feedback Loop: Establish a feedback loop with your team and stakeholders. Continuously gather feedback to

4. Healthcare Analytics:

5. Imaging and Diagnostics:

6. Drug Discovery and Clinical Trials:

7. Electronic Health Records (EHR) and Interoperability:

8. Disaster Recovery and Business Continuity:

9. Collaborative Research:

10. Patient Engagement and Experience:

Section 19.3: GCP in Retail and E-commerce

1. Personalized Shopping Experiences:

2. Inventory Management and Supply Chain Optimization:

3. E-commerce Platforms and Mobile Apps:

4. Fraud Detection and Prevention:

5. Customer Analytics and Insights:

6. Omnichannel Retailing:

7. Point of Sale (POS) Solutions:

8. Customer Support and Chatbots:

9. Recommendations and Personalization:

10. Scalability and Global Reach:

Section 19.4: Media and Entertainment Solutions

1. Content Delivery and Streaming:
2. Media Processing and Transcoding:
3. Content Recommendation and Personalization:
4. Analytics and Viewer Insights:
5. Cloud-Based Editing and Collaboration:
6. Live Streaming and Event Coverage:
7. Archiving and Digital Asset Management:
8. Monetization and Advertising:
9. Content Security and DRM:
10. Interactive Experiences and Augmented Reality (AR):

Section 19.5: GCP for Financial Services and Banking

1. Data Security and Compliance:
2. Data Analytics and Insights:
3. Customer Experience and Personalization:
4. Core Banking and Payment Processing:
5. Regulatory Reporting and Compliance:
6. Fraud Detection and Prevention:
7. Trading and Investment:
8. Asset Management and Wealthtech:

9. Blockchain and Distributed Ledger Technology (DLT):

10. Cloud Cost Management:

Chapter 20: The Future of GCP and Cloud Computing

Section 20.1: Emerging Trends in Cloud Computing

1. Edge Computing and IoT Integration:

2. Serverless Computing and Microservices:

3. AI and Machine Learning Integration:

4. Multi-Cloud and Hybrid Cloud Adoption:

5. Quantum Computing Advancements:

6. Enhanced Security and Privacy:

7. Cloud-Native Development and DevOps:

8. Environmental Sustainability:

9. 5G Integration:

10. Blockchain and Decentralized Applications (DApps):

Section 20.2: Innovations in GCP: What's Next?

1. Advanced AI and Machine Learning Services:

2. Enhanced Data Analytics:

3. AI-Driven Automation:

4. Hybrid and Multi-Cloud Innovations:

5. Serverless and Event-Driven Architectures:
6. Quantum Computing Integration:
7. Enhanced Security Posture:
8. Sustainability Initiatives:
9. Edge Computing Solutions:
10. Community and Collaboration:

Section 20.3: The Role of AI and Machine Learning in Future Cloud Solutions

1. AI-Driven Automation:
2. Enhanced Data Insights:
3. Personalized User Experiences:
4. Advanced Security and Threat Detection:
5. Natural Language Understanding:
6. AutoML and Democratization of AI:
7. Real-Time Decision-Making:
8. AI Ethics and Governance:
9. Quantum Machine Learning:
10. Continuous Innovation:

Section 20.4: Preparing for the Next Wave of Cloud Computing

1. Edge Computing Expansion:

2. Hybrid and Multi-Cloud Adoption:

3. Containerization and Kubernetes:

4. Serverless Computing:

5. AI and ML Integration:

6. Quantum Computing Readiness:

7. Security and Compliance Focus:

8. Cost Optimization Strategies:

9. Resilience and Disaster Recovery:

10. Continuous Learning and Adaptation:

Section 20.5: Conclusion: Embracing the Cloud Future with GCP

1. Cloud Computing's Impact:

2. GCP's Contribution:

3. Continuous Learning:

4. Innovation and Transformation:

5. Security and Compliance:

6. Collaboration and Community:

7. Cost Efficiency:

8. Global Reach:

9. The Future Awaits:

10. Embrace the Cloud Future:

Chapter 1: Introduction to Google Cloud Platform

1.1 The Evolution of Cloud Computing

CLOUD COMPUTING HAS revolutionized the way businesses and individuals manage and store data, access applications, and scale their infrastructure. Over the years, it has evolved significantly to meet the growing demands of the digital age.

The concept of cloud computing traces its roots back to the 1960s when the idea of time-sharing computers emerged. This allowed multiple users to access a single computer simultaneously, a precursor to the modern cloud model. However, it wasn't until the early 2000s that cloud computing as we know it began to take shape.

Virtualization played a pivotal role in the evolution of cloud computing. It allowed multiple virtual machines (VMs) to run on a single physical server, improving resource utilization and flexibility. This technology laid the foundation for the scalable and cost-effective cloud infrastructure we have today.

One of the major milestones in the history of cloud computing was the launch of **Amazon Web Services (AWS)** in 2006. AWS offered on-demand computing resources, such as virtual servers and storage, to anyone with an internet connection. This marked the start of the public cloud era and inspired other tech giants, including Google, to develop their own cloud platforms.

In 2008, Google introduced **Google App Engine**, its first foray into the cloud. App Engine provided a platform for developers to build and deploy web applications without managing the underlying infrastructure. This paved the way for Google's broader cloud offerings.

In 2012, **Google Compute Engine** was launched, providing Infrastructure as a Service (IaaS) with virtual machines. This allowed users to have more control over their cloud resources, making it suitable for a wide range of applications.

Google Cloud Platform (GCP) continued to expand its services, encompassing **storage, networking, databases, machine learning, and more**. It positioned itself as a strong competitor to AWS and other cloud providers, offering unique features and a global network of data centers.

The evolution of cloud computing has not only changed how businesses operate but has also democratized access to cutting-edge technology. It has enabled startups to compete with industry giants, fostered innovation, and reshaped the IT landscape.

As we delve deeper into this book, we will explore the various aspects of Google Cloud Platform (GCP) and how it fits into the broader landscape of cloud computing. We'll examine its core services, compare it with other cloud providers, and discuss its role in modern technology solutions. GCP has come a long way since its inception, and understanding its evolution is essential for harnessing its full potential in today's digital world.

1.2 Overview of Google Cloud Platform (GCP)

GOOGLE CLOUD PLATFORM (GCP) is a comprehensive suite of cloud computing services provided by Google. It offers a wide range of tools and infrastructure for building, deploying, and scaling applications and services. In this section, we will provide an overview of GCP's key features, services, and its position in the cloud market.

Key Features of GCP

1. **Global Network Infrastructure**: GCP boasts one of the largest and most robust global networks, with data centers strategically located around the world. This network infrastructure ensures low-latency access to services and high availability.
2. **Scalability**: GCP allows users to easily scale their resources up or down based on demand. Whether you need more compute power, storage, or network bandwidth, GCP can accommodate your needs.
3. **Security**: Google places a strong emphasis on security. GCP provides a range of security features, including identity and access management (IAM), encryption at rest and in transit, and DDoS protection, to help secure your applications and data.
4. **Big Data and Analytics**: GCP offers a suite of big data and analytics services, including BigQuery for data warehousing, Dataflow for data processing, and Data Studio for data visualization. These tools enable businesses to gain insights from their data.
5. **Machine Learning and AI**: GCP provides a rich set of machine learning and artificial intelligence (AI) services, such as AI Platform, AutoML, and TensorFlow. These services make it easier for developers and data scientists to build and deploy machine learning models.
6. **Serverless Computing**: GCP offers serverless solutions like Cloud Functions and App Engine, which abstract away server management, allowing developers to focus solely on code and application logic.

7. **Containers and Kubernetes**: GCP is known for its strong support for containers and Kubernetes. Google Kubernetes Engine (GKE) simplifies container orchestration and management.

Core GCP Services

GCP'S SERVICES CAN be categorized into several key areas:

1. **Compute**: GCP offers a variety of compute options, including virtual machines (Compute Engine), managed Kubernetes clusters (GKE), and serverless computing (Cloud Functions, App Engine).
2. **Storage**: GCP provides scalable storage solutions such as Cloud Storage for object storage, Cloud SQL and Cloud Spanner for databases, and various data storage options for specific use cases.
3. **Networking**: GCP's networking services include Virtual Private Cloud (VPC), Load Balancers, Cloud DNS, and a global content delivery network (CDN) to ensure reliable and performant network connectivity.
4. **Database and Data Services**: GCP offers a range of database services, from traditional relational databases to NoSQL solutions like Cloud Datastore and Firestore. BigQuery enables advanced data analytics.
5. **Machine Learning and AI**: GCP's AI and machine learning services empower organizations to build and deploy machine learning models, harnessing the power of AI for various applications.
6. **Development Tools**: GCP provides tools for application development, CI/CD (Continuous Integration/ Continuous Deployment), and application monitoring.
7. **Security and Identity**: Identity and Access Management

(IAM), encryption, and security features are integral to GCP's offerings.

8. **Management Tools**: GCP provides tools for managing resources, monitoring performance, and optimizing costs.

GCP in the Cloud Market

GCP IS A MAJOR PLAYER in the cloud market, competing with other cloud providers such as Amazon Web Services (AWS) and Microsoft Azure. It is known for its strengths in areas like data analytics, machine learning, and Kubernetes support. GCP's customers include startups, enterprises, and public sector organizations across various industries.

As we progress through this book, we will dive deeper into each aspect of Google Cloud Platform, exploring how to leverage its services to meet specific business needs and technological challenges. Whether you are a developer, IT professional, or business leader, understanding GCP's capabilities is essential in today's cloud-centric world.

1.3 Comparing GCP with Other Cloud Providers

GOOGLE CLOUD PLATFORM (GCP) is one of several major cloud service providers, each offering a unique set of features, pricing models, and strengths. In this section, we will compare GCP with some of its key competitors, specifically Amazon Web Services (AWS) and Microsoft Azure, to help you understand the distinctions and considerations when choosing a cloud provider.

Market Share and Presence

AWS, GCP, AND AZURE are the three major players in the cloud market. AWS holds the largest market share, followed by Azure, with GCP holding a smaller but steadily growing share. While AWS and Azure have a broader global presence with more regions and availability zones, GCP focuses on expanding its data center locations to meet the needs of its customers.

Pricing Model

EACH CLOUD PROVIDER offers a unique pricing model. GCP employs a billing model called "Pay-as-you-go," where you are charged for the resources you use. AWS and Azure also offer similar models. GCP's pricing is often considered competitive, and it provides sustained use discounts for long-running workloads.

Services and Ecosystem

ALL THREE CLOUD PROVIDERS offer a vast array of services, but they may differ in terms of specific offerings and areas of expertise. GCP is known for its strengths in data analytics, machine learning, and Kubernetes support. AWS has a wide service portfolio and strong developer adoption. Azure is favored by enterprises and offers seamless integration with Microsoft products.

Kubernetes Support

GCP HAS A STRONG EMPHASIS on Kubernetes with its Google Kubernetes Engine (GKE). It provides a managed Kubernetes service that is popular among organizations looking to deploy and manage containerized applications. While AWS and Azure also support Kubernetes, GKE is often praised for its ease of use and strong integration with Kubernetes.

Machine Learning and AI

GCP IS RECOGNIZED FOR its machine learning and artificial intelligence (AI) capabilities, with services like AI Platform, AutoML, and TensorFlow. It provides tools and libraries that make it easier to build and deploy machine learning models. AWS and Azure also have AI and ML offerings, but GCP is known for its leadership in this domain.

Networking and Global Reach

GCP BOASTS A GLOBAL network infrastructure designed for high availability and low-latency connectivity. It has a strong presence in Asia and is known for its performance in these regions. AWS and Azure also have extensive global networks, and the choice may depend on your specific geographical requirements.

Developer Tools and Ecosystem

ALL THREE CLOUD PROVIDERS offer developer tools and support for various programming languages. GCP provides tools like Cloud SDK and Cloud Shell for seamless development and deployment. AWS has a wide developer ecosystem, and Azure offers strong integration with Visual Studio and other Microsoft tools.

Support and Documentation

GCP PROVIDES A RANGE of support options, including community support, basic support, and premium support plans. AWS and Azure offer similar support tiers. All three providers offer extensive documentation, tutorials, and online communities to assist users.

Choosing the Right Cloud Provider

THE CHOICE BETWEEN GCP, AWS, and Azure depends on your organization's specific needs, expertise, and priorities. It's essential to evaluate your requirements, consider factors such as services, pricing, and ecosystem, and possibly conduct proof-of-concept projects to determine the best fit for your cloud strategy.

In this book, we will focus on GCP and explore its capabilities in depth. However, it's valuable to be aware of the differences and comparisons with other cloud providers as you make decisions related to your cloud infrastructure and services.

1.4 Core Services and Capabilities of GCP

GOOGLE CLOUD PLATFORM (GCP) offers a wide range of core services and capabilities designed to meet the diverse needs of businesses and developers. In this section, we will delve into the key services and features that form the foundation of GCP's offerings.

1. Compute Services

GCP PROVIDES SEVERAL compute services to host and manage virtual machines (VMs) and containerized workloads. These include:

- **Compute Engine**: GCP's Infrastructure as a Service (IaaS) offering that allows you to create and manage VMs, giving you full control over the infrastructure.

- **Google Kubernetes Engine (GKE)**: A managed Kubernetes service that simplifies the deployment and scaling of containerized applications.

- **App Engine**: A Platform as a Service (PaaS) that enables developers to build and deploy applications without worrying about infrastructure management.

- **Cloud Functions**: A serverless computing service for executing event-driven functions in response to events or HTTP requests.

2. Storage Services

GCP OFFERS A VARIETY of storage services to handle data storage and retrieval needs:

- **Cloud Storage**: A scalable object storage service suitable for storing and serving static assets, backups, and multimedia content.

- **Cloud SQL**: A managed relational database service compatible with MySQL, PostgreSQL, and SQL Server.

- **Cloud Bigtable**: A high-throughput NoSQL database for large-scale analytical and operational workloads.

- **Cloud Datastore**: A highly available NoSQL database for web and mobile applications.

- **Firestore**: A serverless, scalable NoSQL document database for mobile and web app development.

3. Networking Services

GCP PROVIDES ROBUST networking services for managing connectivity and security:

- **Virtual Private Cloud (VPC)**: A logically isolated network to segment and control network traffic.

- **Load Balancers**: Global load balancing services to distribute traffic across multiple regions and zones for high availability.

- **Cloud DNS**: A scalable and highly available Domain Name System (DNS) service for domain management.

- **Cloud Interconnect**: Enables dedicated network connections between your on-premises network and GCP.

4. Identity and Access Management (IAM)

IAM IS CRUCIAL FOR managing permissions and access control within GCP:

- **Identity and Access Management (IAM)**: A centralized system for defining and managing roles and permissions to control access to GCP resources.

5. Data and Analytics Services

GCP OFFERS A COMPREHENSIVE suite of data and analytics services:

- **BigQuery**: A fully managed, serverless, and highly scalable data warehouse for running fast and SQL-like queries on large datasets.

- **Dataflow**: A managed stream and batch data processing service for building data pipelines.

- **Pub/Sub**: A messaging service for building event-driven systems and real-time analytics.

- **Data Studio**: A data visualization and reporting tool to create interactive dashboards and reports.

6. Machine Learning and AI

GCP PROVIDES POWERFUL machine learning and AI services:

- **AI Platform**: A unified platform for machine learning that offers tools for data preparation, training, and deployment of machine learning models.

- **AutoML**: Enables developers and data scientists to build custom machine learning models with minimal expertise.

- **TensorFlow**: An open-source machine learning framework developed by Google for building and training machine learning models.

7. Developer Tools

GCP OFFERS VARIOUS developer tools to streamline application development and deployment:

- **Cloud SDK**: A set of command-line tools for interacting with GCP services and resources.

- **Cloud Build**: A continuous integration and continuous deployment (CI/CD) service for automating the build and deployment of applications.

8. Management and Monitoring

GCP PROVIDES TOOLS for managing and monitoring your infrastructure:

- **Cloud Resource Manager**: Helps you organize and manage resources across projects.
- **Operations Suite**: Offers monitoring, logging, and diagnostics tools to gain insights into your applications and services.

These core services and capabilities form the foundation upon which you can build, deploy, and manage a wide range of applications and solutions on Google Cloud Platform. In the subsequent chapters of this book, we will explore these services in greater detail, providing hands-on guidance and best practices for leveraging GCP effectively.

1.5 Setting the Stage: GCP's Role in Modern Technology

GOOGLE CLOUD PLATFORM (GCP) has become a pivotal player in modern technology ecosystems, offering a comprehensive suite of cloud services that empower organizations to innovate, scale, and drive digital transformation. In this section, we will discuss the role of GCP in shaping the contemporary technology landscape and how it addresses the evolving needs of businesses and developers.

Enabling Innovation

GCP SERVES AS A CATALYST for innovation by providing access to cutting-edge technologies. Its machine learning and artificial intelligence (AI) capabilities enable businesses to harness the power of data for predictive analytics, natural language processing, and computer vision. This empowers organizations to develop intelligent applications, automate processes, and gain deeper insights into their data.

Supporting Scalability

SCALABILITY IS A FUNDAMENTAL requirement for modern technology solutions, especially in the age of cloud-native applications. GCP's flexible infrastructure allows organizations to scale their resources dynamically, whether it's adding more virtual machines, deploying containerized workloads, or utilizing serverless computing. This adaptability ensures that applications can handle sudden spikes in demand and growth without disruption.

Embracing DevOps and Continuous Delivery

DEVOPS PRACTICES AND continuous delivery have become essential for organizations aiming to accelerate software development and deployment. GCP's integration with tools like Cloud Build and Kubernetes simplifies the implementation of DevOps processes. Developers can automate build and deployment pipelines, enabling faster and more reliable releases.

Facilitating Global Reach

IN TODAY'S INTERCONNECTED world, businesses often need a global presence to serve customers and expand their reach. GCP's extensive network infrastructure, with data centers across the globe, provides low-latency access and redundancy. This global footprint allows organizations to deliver services and applications reliably to users worldwide.

Supporting Diverse Workloads

MODERN TECHNOLOGY ENVIRONMENTS host a diverse range of workloads, from traditional monolithic applications to microservices architectures. GCP's portfolio of services accommodates this diversity, offering solutions for VM-based workloads, containerized applications, serverless functions, and more. Developers have the flexibility to choose the right computing model for their specific use cases.

Enhancing Security and Compliance

SECURITY IS PARAMOUNT in the digital age, with cyber threats constantly evolving. GCP invests heavily in security measures, including encryption, identity and access management, and threat detection. Organizations can leverage GCP's security features to protect their data and applications while ensuring compliance with industry regulations.

Leveraging Open Source Technologies

GCP EMBRACES OPEN-SOURCE technologies and contributes to many open-source projects. Kubernetes, an open-source container orchestration platform initially developed by Google, is a prime example. GCP's strong support for open-source tools and libraries empowers developers to build solutions using the technologies they are familiar with.

Enabling Data-Driven Decisions

DATA HAS BECOME A STRATEGIC asset for businesses, and GCP's data and analytics services help organizations extract value from their data. Whether it's real-time analytics, data warehousing, or machine learning, GCP provides the tools and infrastructure to make data-driven decisions and gain a competitive edge.

In conclusion, Google Cloud Platform plays a vital role in shaping the modern technology landscape by providing the tools and infrastructure needed to drive innovation, scalability, security, and global reach. As we delve deeper into this book, you will gain a deeper understanding of how to harness the capabilities of GCP to build and deploy a wide range of applications and services that meet the demands of the digital era.

Chapter 2: Getting Started with GCP

2.1 Creating a GCP Account

GETTING STARTED WITH Google Cloud Platform (GCP) begins with creating a GCP account. In this section, we will walk you through the steps to create a GCP account, set up billing, and access the GCP Console.

Prerequisites

BEFORE YOU BEGIN, ENSURE you have the following:

- A Google account: If you already have a Gmail or Google Workspace account, you can use it to sign in to GCP. If not, you can create a new Google account.

Steps to Create a GCP Account

1. **Go to the GCP Console**: Open a web browser and go to the Google Cloud Platform Console.
2. **Sign In**: Click on the "Sign in" button in the upper-right corner. Use your existing Google account credentials to sign in. If you don't have a Google account, you can click on the "Create account" link to create one.
3. **Create a Project**: After signing in, you will be prompted to create a project. A project is a logical container for your GCP resources. Enter a project name, select or create an organization, and click "Create."
4. **Enable Billing**: To use GCP services, you need to set up billing. Click on the "Enable billing" button and follow the prompts to enter billing information. Google Cloud offers a free trial with a $300 credit, so you can explore many

services without incurring charges initially.

5. **Accept Terms and Conditions**: Review and accept the terms and conditions to complete the billing setup.
6. **Verify Your Identity**: Google may require you to verify your identity for security purposes. Follow the on-screen instructions to complete the verification process.
7. **Access the GCP Console**: Once your account is set up and billing is enabled, you can access the GCP Console by clicking on the "Go to the console" button.

Exploring the GCP Console

THE GCP CONSOLE IS your central hub for managing GCP resources and services. Here are some key features and sections of the console:

- **Navigation Menu**: The left-side navigation menu provides access to various GCP services, including Compute Engine, Storage, Networking, and more.

- **Dashboard**: The dashboard gives you an overview of your project's resources, recent activity, and access to important links.

- **Resource Hierarchy**: GCP uses a resource hierarchy to organize resources within a project. You can explore and manage resources under "IAM & Admin" > "Resource Hierarchy."

- **Billing**: You can monitor your billing and usage by navigating to "Billing" in the navigation menu.

- **IAM & Admin**: This section allows you to manage permissions and access control for your GCP project.

Congratulations! You've successfully created a GCP account, set up billing, and accessed the GCP Console. You are now ready to explore GCP's core services, build applications, and harness the power of the cloud for your projects.

2.2 Navigating the GCP Console

ONCE YOU'VE CREATED your Google Cloud Platform (GCP) account, it's essential to become familiar with the GCP Console, as it's where you'll manage your GCP resources, services, and projects. In this section, we will explore the GCP Console's interface and guide you through its essential elements.

The GCP Console Interface

WHEN YOU ACCESS THE GCP Console, you'll be greeted by a user-friendly interface designed to help you manage and interact with GCP services effectively. Here are some key components of the GCP Console:

1. **Navigation Menu**: Located on the left side of the console, the navigation menu provides access to various GCP services and resources. You can expand sections to view and access specific services, such as Compute Engine, Storage, Networking, and more.
2. **Search Bar**: At the top of the console, there's a search bar that allows you to quickly find resources, services, and documentation. You can use this feature to locate specific GCP resources or access relevant documentation.
3. **Dashboard**: The dashboard is the default landing page when you log in. It provides an overview of your GCP project's current status, including recent activity, billing information, and access to key links and resources.

4. **Project Selector**: In the top-left corner of the console, you'll find the project selector. This allows you to switch between different GCP projects if you have multiple projects associated with your account.
5. **Notifications**: Notifications and alerts related to your GCP resources and account are displayed on the top-right corner of the console. It's essential to monitor these notifications to stay informed about any important updates or issues.
6. **Help and Documentation**: The "Help" menu provides access to GCP documentation, support, and community resources. It's a valuable source of information when you have questions or need assistance.

Navigating the GCP Console

HERE'S A BRIEF GUIDE on how to navigate and use the GCP Console effectively:

1. **Select a Project**: If you have multiple projects, use the project selector to choose the project you want to work on. Your active project determines which resources and services are available for management.
2. **Navigation Menu**: Explore the navigation menu to access specific GCP services and resources. Click on a service to open its dashboard or configuration settings.
3. **Dashboard**: The dashboard provides an overview of your project's status. You can see recent activity, billing information, and quick links to important sections. It's a great starting point for monitoring your GCP resources.
4. **Resource Hierarchy**: GCP uses a resource hierarchy to organize and manage resources within a project. You can access this hierarchy under "IAM & Admin" in the

navigation menu. It helps you visualize the structure of your GCP project.

5. **Search Bar**: Use the search bar at the top of the console to quickly find specific GCP resources, services, or documentation. Simply type keywords or resource names, and relevant results will be displayed.
6. **Help and Documentation**: When you need assistance or information, click on the "Help" menu to access GCP documentation, support options, and community resources. It's a valuable reference for troubleshooting and learning.
7. **Notifications**: Keep an eye on notifications and alerts in the top-right corner. These notifications can provide critical information about your GCP resources and account.

The GCP Console is your central hub for managing and interacting with GCP services. As you explore and work with GCP, you'll become more comfortable with its interface and tools, making it easier to build, deploy, and manage cloud-based applications and resources for your projects.

2.3 Understanding Billing and Pricing Models

TO EFFECTIVELY USE Google Cloud Platform (GCP), it's crucial to understand the billing and pricing models associated with GCP services. In this section, we will explore how GCP charges for its services, common pricing considerations, and tools available to help you manage costs.

Billing Accounts and Billing Reports

WHEN YOU CREATE A GCP account, you are required to set up a billing account. A billing account is associated with a specific payment method and is used to pay for the usage of GCP services. It's essential to manage billing accounts properly, especially if you have multiple projects or organizations.

Billing Reports

GCP PROVIDES DETAILED billing reports that offer insights into your usage and expenditures. These reports are accessible from the GCP Console and can help you track costs, identify usage trends, and allocate expenses. You can create custom reports to suit your needs.

Pricing Models

GCP OFFERS VARIOUS pricing models for its services, and understanding these models is crucial for cost management. Here are some common pricing models used by GCP:

1. **Pay-as-You-Go**: Many GCP services follow a pay-as-you-go model, where you are billed based on your actual usage. This model provides flexibility and cost-effectiveness, as you only pay for what you use.
2. **Sustained Use Discounts**: GCP offers discounts for long-running workloads. If you consistently use a virtual machine (VM) instance, you may qualify for automatic discounts based on the instance's monthly usage.
3. **Committed Use Discounts**: With committed use contracts, you commit to using a specific amount of resources for a one or three-year term. In exchange, you

receive significant discounts on the resources you commit to.

4. **Free Tier**: GCP provides a free tier that includes a limited amount of usage for many of its services. This allows you to explore and experiment with GCP services without incurring charges.
5. **Custom Pricing**: For some services, particularly enterprise solutions or high-usage scenarios, custom pricing may be available. You can work with Google Cloud sales representatives to negotiate custom pricing agreements.

Cost Estimation and Billing Tools

GCP OFFERS SEVERAL tools to help you estimate and manage costs:

1. **Pricing Calculator**: The GCP Pricing Calculator is a web-based tool that allows you to estimate the cost of using GCP services based on your expected usage. It helps you plan and budget for your projects.
2. **Budgets and Alerts**: GCP allows you to set budget thresholds and receive alerts when your spending approaches or exceeds those thresholds. This feature helps you stay within your budget and avoid unexpected expenses.
3. **Cost Explorer**: Cost Explorer is a feature within the GCP Console that provides visualizations and insights into your spending patterns. It helps you understand your cost breakdown and identify areas where you can optimize spending.

Cost Optimization Best Practices

TO EFFECTIVELY MANAGE costs on GCP, consider the following best practices:

- **Regularly review billing reports**: Periodically review your billing reports to monitor usage and expenses. Look for trends or areas where cost optimization is possible.

- **Use quotas and limits**: Set resource quotas and limits to prevent unexpected overages. This can help control spending and ensure you stay within your budget.

- **Utilize automation**: Leverage automation tools and scripts to start and stop resources as needed. This can help reduce costs by only running resources when necessary.

- **Monitor and adjust**: Continuously monitor your GCP resources and adjust configurations based on changing requirements. For example, resize VM instances or scale down underutilized resources.

- **Leverage managed services**: Consider using GCP's managed services, such as Google Kubernetes Engine (GKE) or Cloud Functions, which automatically handle resource scaling and optimization.

- **Explore cost-effective regions**: GCP offers different pricing for resources in different regions. Consider deploying resources in regions with lower pricing if it aligns with your application's requirements.

Effective cost management is an essential aspect of using GCP efficiently. By understanding the billing and pricing models, using cost estimation tools, and implementing cost optimization best practices, you can effectively control and optimize your GCP spending while getting the most value out of the platform.

2.4 Setting Up Your First Project

CREATING A GCP PROJECT is one of the initial steps to begin using Google Cloud Platform effectively. In this section, we will guide you through the process of setting up your first GCP project and provide insights into project organization and management.

What is a GCP Project?

A GCP PROJECT IS A logical container that helps you organize and manage your GCP resources, services, and applications. Projects are used to isolate resources, control access, and track billing and usage. When you create a GCP account, you automatically have a default project, but you can create additional projects to suit your needs.

Creating a GCP Project

HERE'S HOW TO CREATE your first GCP project:

1. **Access the GCP Console**: Log in to your GCP account and access the GCP Console by visiting https://console.cloud.google.com/.
2. **Project Selector**: In the top-left corner of the console, click on the project selector. This dropdown allows you to switch between existing projects or create a new one.
3. **Create a Project**: To create a new project, click on the "New Project" button.
4. **Project Details**: You will be prompted to provide some details for your project:

– **Project Name**: Choose a descriptive name for your project.

– **Organization**: If you are part of an organization, you can select it here. Otherwise, choose "No organization."

1. **Billing Information**: Next, you will be asked to link a billing account to your project. If you haven't set up billing yet, you will need to do so at this stage.
2. **Location**: Optionally, you can choose a location for your project. This can affect the location of certain resources and services, but it's not required.
3. **Create**: After filling in the necessary information, click the "Create" button to create your project.

Project Organization and Management

ONCE YOUR PROJECT IS created, you can start managing and organizing your resources within it. Here are some important aspects of project organization:

• **Resource Hierarchy**: GCP uses a resource hierarchy that includes organizations, folders, and projects. Projects are organized within folders, and folders are part of an organization. This hierarchy helps manage access control and resource organization.

• **IAM & Admin**: The "IAM & Admin" section in the GCP Console allows you to manage permissions and access control for your project. You can assign roles and permissions to users and service accounts.

• **Service Usage**: In the "Service Usage" section, you can enable or disable specific GCP services for your project.

This allows you to control which services are available to your applications.

• **Billing**: You can monitor and manage billing for your project in the "Billing" section. This includes viewing usage, setting budgets, and managing billing accounts.

Best Practices for Project Management

HERE ARE SOME BEST practices for managing GCP projects effectively:

• **Naming Conventions**: Use descriptive and consistent naming conventions for your projects to make it easier to identify their purpose.

• **Resource Labels**: Use labels to categorize and organize resources within your project. Labels are key-value pairs that can help with resource tracking and cost allocation.

• **Permissions and Access Control**: Implement the principle of least privilege when assigning roles and permissions. Only grant access to the resources and services necessary for each user or service account.

• **Resource Cleanup**: Regularly review and clean up resources that are no longer needed to avoid unnecessary charges.

• **Monitoring and Alerts**: Set up monitoring and alerting to be notified of any unusual activity or resource utilization in your project.

Setting up your first GCP project is a fundamental step in leveraging GCP's cloud capabilities for your applications and services. By following best practices for project organization and management, you can ensure a well-structured and secure environment for your cloud-based projects.

2.5 Essential GCP Resources and Support

GOOGLE CLOUD PLATFORM (GCP) offers a wide array of resources and support options to help users navigate and make the most of the platform. In this section, we'll explore essential GCP resources and support channels that are valuable for users at all levels.

GCP Documentation

GCP PROVIDES COMPREHENSIVE documentation that covers all aspects of the platform. The documentation includes detailed guides, tutorials, reference materials, and code samples. Whether you're a beginner exploring GCP or an experienced user looking for specific information, the documentation is a valuable resource.

You can access the GCP documentation at https://cloud.google.com/docs.

GCP Console Help

THE GCP CONSOLE ITSELF is equipped with built-in help and documentation features. You can find helpful information and links to relevant documentation directly within the console. Clicking on the question mark icon or "Learn more" links will provide context-specific guidance.

Google Cloud Community

THE GOOGLE CLOUD COMMUNITY is an online forum where users can seek help, share knowledge, and discuss GCP-related topics. It's a valuable platform for getting answers to your questions, sharing experiences, and connecting with other GCP users and experts.

You can access the Google Cloud Community at https://cloud.google.com/community.

Google Cloud Blogs

GOOGLE MAINTAINS A blog that provides updates, news, and insights related to GCP and cloud computing in general. Reading the blog can keep you informed about the latest developments, best practices, and real-world use cases.

You can access the Google Cloud Blog at https://cloud.google.com/blog.

Google Cloud YouTube Channel

GOOGLE CLOUD HAS AN official YouTube channel where you can find videos, tutorials, webinars, and presentations related to GCP services and solutions. Visual content can be a great way to learn and stay updated on GCP topics.

You can access the Google Cloud YouTube channel at https://www.youtube.com/user/googlecloud.

Google Cloud Support

FOR BUSINESSES AND organizations with specific needs and requirements, Google Cloud offers various levels of support. These support packages provide access to technical support engineers, 24/7 availability, and response time guarantees. Google Cloud Support is essential for mission-critical applications and enterprises.

You can learn more about Google Cloud Support at https://cloud.google.com/support.

GCP Status Dashboard

THE GCP STATUS DASHBOARD provides real-time information about the status of GCP services and regions. It's an essential resource for checking the health and availability of GCP services and diagnosing potential issues.

You can access the GCP Status Dashboard at https://status.cloud.google.com/.

Training and Certification

GOOGLE CLOUD OFFERS training and certification programs for individuals and organizations. These programs allow you to gain expertise in GCP and demonstrate your knowledge through certification exams. Google Cloud certification is recognized in the industry and can enhance your career prospects.

You can explore Google Cloud training and certification at https://cloud.google.com/training.

Cloud Marketplace

THE GCP MARKETPLACE is a platform where you can discover and deploy pre-configured solutions, including software, services, and APIs, from Google and its partners. It's a convenient way to find and use third-party solutions that integrate seamlessly with GCP.

You can explore the GCP Marketplace at https://console.cloud.google.com/marketplace.

These essential GCP resources and support channels are valuable assets for anyone working with Google Cloud Platform. Whether you're seeking documentation, community help, expert support, or training, GCP offers a rich ecosystem to support your cloud journey.

Chapter 3: Core Infrastructure Services

3.1 Exploring Compute Engine

GOOGLE CLOUD PLATFORM'S (GCP) Compute Engine is a fundamental service that allows you to create and manage virtual machines (VMs) in the cloud. In this section, we'll delve into Compute Engine and understand how it works, its key features, and how to get started with creating and managing VMs.

Understanding Compute Engine

COMPUTE ENGINE IS GCP'S Infrastructure as a Service (IaaS) offering, providing scalable and flexible virtual machine instances that run in Google's data centers. It enables you to create and customize VMs based on your computing needs, whether you require a single VM for a specific task or a large cluster for high-performance computing.

Key Features of Compute Engine

- **Choice of Operating Systems**: Compute Engine supports a wide range of operating systems, including Linux and Windows. You can choose from various distributions and versions to meet your requirements.

- **Custom Machine Types**: You can create custom VM instances with the precise CPU and memory configurations you need, allowing you to optimize performance and cost.

- **Predefined Machine Types**: Compute Engine offers predefined machine types optimized for various workloads, such as general-purpose, memory-optimized, and compute-optimized instances.

• **Persistent Disks**: Compute Engine provides persistent block storage disks that can be attached to VMs. These disks can be used for booting instances and storing data.

• **Load Balancing**: Compute Engine includes load balancing options to distribute incoming traffic across multiple VM instances, ensuring high availability and fault tolerance.

• **Snapshots and Images**: You can create snapshots of VM disks and use them to create custom images. This is useful for backup, cloning, and creating templates for VM instances.

• **Auto Scaling**: Compute Engine allows you to set up auto-scaling based on predefined policies, ensuring that your application can handle varying levels of traffic.

Getting Started with Compute Engine

HERE'S A BASIC OVERVIEW of how to get started with Compute Engine:

1. **Access the GCP Console**: Log in to your GCP account and access the GCP Console.
2. **Navigate to Compute Engine**: In the GCP Console, select "Compute Engine" from the left-side navigation menu to access Compute Engine-related resources.
3. **Creating a VM Instance**: To create a VM instance, click the "Create" button. You will be prompted to configure various settings, including the instance name, machine

type, boot disk, and more. Follow the prompts to create your VM.

4. **SSH Access**: Once your VM is created, you can use SSH to access it. GCP provides a browser-based SSH terminal for easy access, or you can use third-party SSH clients.
5. **Managing VMs**: You can start, stop, delete, or modify your VM instances as needed using the GCP Console or the command-line tools.
6. **Billing and Monitoring**: Keep an eye on your billing and monitor resource usage through the GCP Console to ensure cost-effective operation.

Use Cases for Compute Engine

COMPUTE ENGINE IS VERSATILE and can be used for various use cases, including:

- Hosting web applications and websites.
- Running containerized workloads with Kubernetes.
- Performing data analysis and machine learning tasks.
- Running batch processing and data pipelines.
- Hosting game servers and real-time applications.
- Handling high-performance computing (HPC) workloads.

Compute Engine's flexibility and scalability make it a core component of many cloud-based applications and services. Understanding how to leverage Compute Engine effectively is essential for building and managing your cloud infrastructure.

3.2 Storage Options in GCP: Cloud Storage, Filestore, and More

GOOGLE CLOUD PLATFORM (GCP) offers a variety of storage options to cater to different data storage and retrieval needs. In this section, we'll explore key storage services provided by GCP, including Google Cloud Storage and Cloud Filestore, and understand how they can be used in different scenarios.

Google Cloud Storage

GOOGLE CLOUD STORAGE is a highly scalable and durable object storage service that allows you to store and retrieve data in a flexible and cost-effective manner. Here are some key features and use cases of Google Cloud Storage:

Key Features:

- **Multi-Regional and Regional Buckets**: You can choose the location of your storage buckets to optimize latency, availability, and compliance. Google Cloud Storage offers multi-regional, regional, and dual-regional storage classes.

- **Scalability**: Google Cloud Storage can handle massive amounts of data and is designed for scalability. You can easily scale your storage as your needs grow.

- **Data Lifecycle Management**: You can set up lifecycle policies to automatically manage the lifecycle of your objects, including archiving or deleting them based on predefined rules.

• **Security**: Data stored in Google Cloud Storage is encrypted at rest by default. You can also enable encryption in transit and control access using Identity and Access Management (IAM) policies.

• **Integration**: Google Cloud Storage integrates seamlessly with other GCP services, such as BigQuery, Dataflow, and Cloud Pub/Sub, making it a versatile choice for data storage in cloud-native applications.

Use Cases:

• **Object Storage**: Google Cloud Storage is ideal for storing objects, such as images, videos, backups, and documents. It can serve as a content repository for web applications and mobile apps.

• **Data Lake**: It can be used as a data lake for storing large volumes of structured and unstructured data, which can be analyzed using GCP's analytics and machine learning services.

• **Backup and Archive**: Google Cloud Storage's archival storage class is suitable for long-term data retention and backup strategies.

Cloud Filestore

CLOUD FILESTORE IS a managed file storage service designed for applications that require a shared file system. It provides a high-performance, fully managed network-attached storage (NAS) solution. Here are its key features and use cases:

Key Features:

- **High Performance**: Cloud Filestore offers high throughput and low latency, making it suitable for applications that require high-speed file access.

- **Managed Service**: It is fully managed, meaning you don't have to worry about server management, updates, or scaling.

- **SMB and NFS Support**: Cloud Filestore supports both the SMB (Server Message Block) and NFS (Network File System) protocols, making it compatible with a wide range of applications and operating systems.

- **Snapshots**: You can create snapshots of your file shares to capture point-in-time backups for data recovery.

Use Cases:

- **Shared File Storage**: Cloud Filestore is ideal for applications that require shared file storage, such as content management systems (CMS), development environments, and home directories.

- **Media and Entertainment**: It can be used for rendering and content delivery workflows in the media and entertainment industry.

- **Data Processing**: Cloud Filestore is suitable for data processing tasks that involve shared access to input and output data.

Additional Storage Services

IN ADDITION TO GOOGLE Cloud Storage and Cloud Filestore, GCP offers a range of other storage services, including:

- **Cloud SQL**: Managed relational databases with options for MySQL, PostgreSQL, and SQL Server.
- **Cloud Bigtable**: A fully managed NoSQL database service for large analytical and operational workloads.
- **Firestore**: A serverless, NoSQL document database for web, mobile, and server applications.
- **Cloud Spanner**: A globally distributed, horizontally scalable, and strongly consistent database service.
- **Persistent Disks**: Block storage that can be attached to Compute Engine instances.

These storage options in GCP cater to various data storage and retrieval needs, from object storage and file sharing to databases and NoSQL solutions. Choosing the right storage service depends on your specific use case, scalability requirements, and performance expectations.

3.3 Networking in GCP: VPC, Load Balancers, and Cloud DNS

GOOGLE CLOUD PLATFORM (GCP) provides robust networking capabilities to build and manage your cloud infrastructure. In this section, we'll explore key networking components, including Virtual Private Cloud (VPC), Load

Balancers, and Cloud DNS, and understand how they facilitate network management and traffic distribution.

Virtual Private Cloud (VPC)

VIRTUAL PRIVATE CLOUD (VPC) is a foundational networking service in GCP that allows you to create and manage isolated network environments. Each VPC is a logically isolated section of GCP's global network, providing control over IP addressing, routing, and firewall policies. Here are the key features and use cases of VPC:

Key Features:

- **Isolation**: VPCs provide network isolation, allowing you to create distinct network segments for different applications or projects.

- **Custom IP Ranges**: You can define custom IP address ranges for your VPC, providing flexibility in addressing and subnetting.

- **Firewall Rules**: VPCs enable you to define firewall rules to control incoming and outgoing traffic to your virtual machines (VMs) and services.

- **Private Google Access**: VMs within a VPC can securely access Google services like Cloud Storage and BigQuery without exposing them to the public internet.

- **Global Routing**: VPCs offer global routing tables, allowing traffic to flow seamlessly across regions and zones within a VPC.

Use Cases:

- **Application Isolation**: Use VPCs to isolate applications, development, and test environments, ensuring they don't interfere with each other.
- **Security Segmentation**: Create separate VPCs to segment traffic for security and compliance reasons, implementing different firewall policies as needed.
- **Hybrid Cloud Connectivity**: Establish VPN or Interconnect connections to extend your on-premises network into GCP VPCs, creating hybrid cloud environments.

Load Balancers

GCP PROVIDES LOAD BALANCING solutions to distribute traffic evenly among multiple virtual machines (VMs) or instances, ensuring high availability and reliability of applications. Here are the key load balancing options in GCP:

Key Load Balancing Services:

- **HTTP(S) Load Balancing**: Designed for internet-facing web applications, it offers SSL/TLS termination and global routing for HTTP/HTTPS traffic.
- **TCP/UDP Load Balancing**: For non-HTTP traffic, it balances TCP and UDP traffic across backend instances in multiple regions.

- **Internal Load Balancing**: Used to balance internal traffic within a VPC, ensuring high availability of services.

- **Network Load Balancing**: Distributes traffic at the network layer, handling high-throughput and low-latency workloads.

Use Cases:

- **High Availability**: Use load balancers to ensure that your applications remain available even if individual instances fail.

- **Scaling**: Automatically scale your application by adding or removing instances based on traffic load.

- **Global Reach**: HTTP(S) Load Balancing offers global distribution, making it suitable for applications with users worldwide.

Cloud DNS

CLOUD DNS IS A SCALABLE and highly available Domain Name System (DNS) service that enables you to manage domain names and resolve them into IP addresses. It offers both public and private DNS zones for your applications. Here are the key features and use cases of Cloud DNS:

Key Features:

- **Zone Management**: Create and manage DNS zones for your domains.

- **Global Anycast**: Cloud DNS uses a global anycast network to provide low-latency and highly available DNS resolution.

- **Integration**: It integrates seamlessly with other GCP services and external services.

Use Cases:

- **Domain Management**: Use Cloud DNS to manage domain names for your websites and applications.

- **Service Discovery**: Facilitate service discovery by associating DNS names with the IP addresses of backend services.

- **Private DNS**: Create private DNS zones for internal applications and services, ensuring secure and isolated DNS resolution.

THESE NETWORKING COMPONENTS, including VPCs, Load Balancers, and Cloud DNS, are crucial for designing and managing a robust and scalable network infrastructure in GCP. Whether you need to isolate applications, distribute traffic, or manage domain names, GCP's networking services provide the flexibility and reliability required for modern cloud-based applications.

3.4 Identity and Access Management (IAM)

IDENTITY AND ACCESS Management (IAM) is a crucial aspect of managing security and access control in Google Cloud Platform (GCP). IAM allows you to define who can access GCP resources and what actions they can perform. In this section, we'll explore IAM concepts, roles, and best practices for securing your GCP environment.

IAM Concepts

1. Identity: An identity can be a user, a group, or a service account that is used to represent individuals, teams, or applications. Each identity is associated with a Google Account or a Google Workspace domain.

2. Resource: A resource in GCP can be anything you want to control access to, such as virtual machines, storage buckets, databases, and more.

3. Role: A role defines a set of permissions that specify what actions can be performed on a resource. Roles are assigned to identities to control access.

4. Policy: A policy binds a role to a resource, indicating which identities have what level of access to that resource. Policies are defined at the project, folder, or organization level.

IAM Roles

GCP PROVIDES A SET of predefined roles with specific permissions that you can assign to identities. Here are some common predefined roles:

- **Owner**: Has full control over resources and IAM policies, including the ability to grant or revoke access to others.

- **Editor**: Can modify resources and IAM policies but can't manage identities.

- **Viewer**: Can view resources and access read-only APIs.

- **IAM roles related to specific services**: Many GCP services have their own predefined roles, such as "Storage Admin" for Google Cloud Storage or "BigQuery Admin" for BigQuery.

IAM Best Practices

1. Use the Principle of Least Privilege: Assign the minimum permissions necessary to perform a specific task. Avoid granting broad permissions like "Owner" unless absolutely necessary.

2. Regularly Review and Update Permissions: As your environment evolves, periodically review and adjust permissions to align with the changing requirements of your team or project.

3. Implement a Strong Identity Management Strategy: Use groups and service accounts to manage access efficiently. Avoid assigning permissions directly to individual users whenever possible.

4. Enable Auditing and Monitoring: Use Cloud Audit Logs and Cloud Monitoring to track access and detect suspicious activities.

5. Apply IAM Policies Hierarchically: IAM policies can be defined at the organization, folder, and project levels. Define policies at the highest level possible to simplify access management.

IAM in Action

HERE'S AN EXAMPLE OF how IAM can be applied to a GCP resource:

Suppose you have a Cloud Storage bucket that contains sensitive data. You can create an IAM policy that grants "Read" permission to a specific group of users who need access and "Owner" permission to a service account used by an application that writes data to the bucket. You would apply this policy to the bucket to control access effectively.

```
# Define an IAM policy in JSON format
{
"bindings": [
{
"role": "roles/storage.objectViewer",
"members": [
"group:project-team@example.com"
]
},
{
"role": "roles/storage.objectOwner",
"members": [
"serviceAccount:app-service@your-project-id.iam.gserviceaccount.com"
]
}
]
}
```

IAM is a fundamental component of GCP's security model, enabling you to manage access and permissions in a fine-grained manner. By following IAM best practices and applying role-based access control, you can enhance the security and compliance of your GCP environment.

3.5 Managing Resources with Cloud Resource Manager

GOOGLE CLOUD RESOURCE Manager is a service that helps you organize and manage your GCP resources efficiently. It allows you to create and manage projects, folders, and organizations, providing a structured approach to resource management. In this section, we'll explore how Cloud Resource Manager can help you maintain control and organization over your GCP environment.

Organizational Hierarchy

AT THE TOP OF THE HIERARCHY is the **organization**, representing your entire company or entity. Under the organization, you can create **folders** to group resources based on your organizational structure, such as departments or teams. Within folders, you can create **projects** to manage specific GCP resources, services, and billing.

Key Concepts

1. Organization: Represents your entire company or entity. It provides a central place for managing policies and permissions across your GCP environment.

2. Folder: Folders are used to group projects and resources. They allow you to apply policies and permissions to multiple projects at once.

3. Project: Projects are used to organize and manage GCP resources, including VM instances, databases, and storage buckets. Each project has its own billing and access controls.

Benefits of Using Cloud Resource Manager

1. Policy and Access Control: Cloud Resource Manager enables you to apply IAM policies and permissions at the organization, folder, or project level. This fine-grained control helps you manage access and permissions effectively.

2. Cost Management: You can associate projects with billing accounts, allowing you to track and manage costs for different teams or departments within your organization.

3. Resource Organization: The hierarchical structure of Cloud Resource Manager helps you organize your GCP resources logically, making it easier to manage and locate resources.

4. Centralized Management: You can centrally manage policies, IAM roles, and other configurations across your organization, ensuring consistent security and compliance.

Using Cloud Resource Manager

HERE'S AN EXAMPLE OF how you can create a folder within your organization using the gcloud command-line tool:

Create a folder

gcloud resource-manager folders create FOLDER_ID \

—display-name "Folder Display Name" \

—organization=ORGANIZATION_ID

In the above command, replace FOLDER_ID with the desired folder ID, "Folder Display Name" with the display name you want, and ORGANIZATION_ID with your organization's ID.

Best Practices

TO MAKE THE MOST OF Cloud Resource Manager, consider the following best practices:

1. Reflect Your Organization's Structure: Create folders and projects that mirror your organization's departments, teams, or business units. This makes resource management more intuitive.

2. Use IAM Roles: Apply IAM roles and permissions at the folder and project levels to control access and permissions effectively.

3. Billing Controls: Associate projects with billing accounts to track and manage costs for specific teams or projects.

4. Regular Review: Periodically review and clean up unused or unnecessary folders and projects to optimize resource allocation and costs.

CLOUD RESOURCE MANAGER is a powerful tool for structuring and managing your GCP resources, providing organization, control, and security across your cloud environment. By adopting a well-organized approach to resource management, you can streamline operations and ensure that your GCP environment aligns with your organization's structure and objectives.

Chapter 4: Data Management and Databases

4.1 Introduction to Big Data in GCP

GOOGLE CLOUD PLATFORM (GCP) offers a comprehensive suite of tools and services for managing and analyzing large datasets, commonly referred to as Big Data. In this section, we'll explore the concept of Big Data, its challenges, and how GCP provides solutions for storing, processing, and analyzing vast amounts of data efficiently.

What is Big Data?

BIG DATA REFERS TO datasets that are too large, complex, or rapidly changing for traditional data processing tools and methods to handle effectively. These datasets often exhibit characteristics known as the "Three Vs":

1. **Volume**: Big Data involves massive volumes of data, often terabytes, petabytes, or more, generated from various sources, including sensors, social media, and applications.
2. **Velocity**: Data is generated at high speeds, requiring real-time or near-real-time processing and analysis to extract insights and make informed decisions.
3. **Variety**: Big Data comes in various formats, including structured data (like databases), semi-structured data (like JSON or XML), and unstructured data (like text, images, or videos).

Challenges of Big Data

MANAGING AND DERIVING value from Big Data pose several challenges:

- **Storage**: Storing vast amounts of data efficiently and cost-effectively can be complex, especially when dealing with diverse data formats.

- **Processing**: Traditional data processing tools may not scale to handle the volume and velocity of Big Data.

- **Analysis**: Extracting meaningful insights and patterns from large datasets requires advanced analytical techniques.

- **Security**: Ensuring the security and privacy of sensitive data is critical, particularly when dealing with vast datasets.

- **Cost Optimization**: Controlling costs while scaling resources to meet Big Data demands is a continuous challenge.

GCP's Big Data Solutions

GCP PROVIDES A RANGE of Big Data solutions to address these challenges:

1. BigQuery: Google's fully managed, serverless data warehouse for running super-fast SQL queries. It's designed for analytical workloads and can handle petabytes of data.

2. Dataflow: A fully managed stream and batch data processing

service that supports real-time data analysis and ETL (Extract, Transform, Load) tasks.

3. Dataprep: A data preparation service that helps clean, structure, and enrich your data before analysis.

4. Bigtable: A NoSQL database service for managing and analyzing large datasets with low-latency access.

5. Pub/Sub: A messaging service for building event-driven systems and real-time data processing pipelines.

6. Cloud Storage: Scalable object storage for storing and serving large datasets.

Getting Started with Big Data in GCP

TO START WORKING WITH Big Data in GCP, you can create a project and select the relevant GCP services based on your specific needs. For example, if you need to analyze large datasets using SQL, BigQuery would be a suitable choice. If you have streaming data that requires real-time processing, Dataflow and Pub/Sub may be more appropriate.

```
# Creating a GCP project using gcloud command-line tool

gcloud projects create PROJECT_ID
```

Big Data in GCP opens up opportunities for organizations to gain valuable insights from their data, make data-driven decisions, and stay competitive in today's data-rich landscape. Whether you're dealing with large-scale analytics, real-time processing, or data warehousing, GCP's Big Data solutions provide the tools and infrastructure needed to tackle the challenges of managing and analyzing Big Data effectively.

4.2 Working with BigQuery for Data Warehousing

BIGQUERY IS GOOGLE Cloud Platform's fully managed, serverless data warehousing and analytics service. It enables you to analyze large datasets quickly and cost-effectively using SQL queries. In this section, we'll explore the key features and use cases of BigQuery and how to get started with it.

Key Features of BigQuery

1. Serverless: BigQuery is a serverless service, meaning you don't need to manage infrastructure, perform capacity planning, or worry about scaling. Google takes care of these aspects, allowing you to focus on data analysis.

2. Fully Managed: It is a fully managed service, including automated backups, high availability, and security. You can trust Google to handle the operational aspects.

3. Scalable: BigQuery can handle massive datasets, ranging from gigabytes to petabytes, and scales automatically as your data grows. You only pay for the queries and storage you use.

4. Standard SQL: BigQuery uses standard SQL for querying data, making it accessible to users with SQL expertise. You can run complex analytical queries with ease.

5. Integration: It integrates seamlessly with other GCP services like Cloud Storage, Dataflow, and Cloud Dataprep, allowing you to build end-to-end data pipelines.

6. Real-time Analysis: You can run real-time analysis on streaming data with BigQuery's support for streaming inserts and queries.

Use Cases of BigQuery

BIGQUERY IS VERSATILE and can be used for various data analysis scenarios:

1. Business Intelligence: Create dashboards and reports to gain insights into your business data.

2. Data Warehousing: Store and query large datasets for historical analysis.

3. Log Analysis: Analyze logs and event data in real-time for troubleshooting and monitoring.

4. Machine Learning: Use BigQuery ML to build and train machine learning models on your data.

5. Predictive Analytics: Perform predictive analytics by applying machine learning models to historical data.

Getting Started with BigQuery

TO GET STARTED WITH BigQuery, follow these steps:

1. **Create a GCP Project**: If you haven't already, create a GCP project where you will use BigQuery.

```
# Creating a GCP project using gcloud command-line tool

gcloud projects create PROJECT_ID
```

1. **Enable the BigQuery API**: In your GCP project, enable the BigQuery API.

```
gcloud services enable bigquery.googleapis.com—project=PROJECT_ID
```

1. **Install the BigQuery Client**: You can use the bq command-line tool or client libraries to interact with BigQuery. Install the bq tool if you prefer the command line.

```
# Install the BigQuery command-line tool

gcloud components install bq
```

1. **Authenticate**: Authenticate your account with Google Cloud to access BigQuery.

```
gcloud auth login
```

1. **Create a Dataset**: Create a dataset within BigQuery to organize your tables and data.

```
# Creating a dataset

bq mk DATASET_NAME
```

1. **Load Data**: Load your data into BigQuery tables. You can use various methods, including batch loading and streaming.

```
# Loading data from a CSV file

bq load DATASET_NAME.TABLE_NAME path/to/your/data.csv
```

1. **Query Data**: Start querying your data using SQL queries.

```
# Running a SQL query

bq query—nouse_legacy_sql 'SELECT * FROM DATASET_NAME.TABLE_NAME WHERE column_name = "value"'
```

BigQuery offers a web UI, command-line tools, and client libraries for various programming languages, making it accessible to data analysts, engineers, and data scientists. It's a powerful tool for data warehousing and analytics in the cloud, allowing you to derive valuable insights from your data quickly and efficiently.

4.3 Database Services: Cloud SQL and Cloud Spanner

GOOGLE CLOUD PLATFORM (GCP) provides two powerful managed database services, Cloud SQL and Cloud Spanner, each tailored for specific use cases. In this section, we'll explore these services, their features, and when to choose one over the other.

Cloud SQL

CLOUD SQL IS A FULLY managed relational database service that supports popular database engines like MySQL, PostgreSQL, and SQL Server. It is an excellent choice for traditional relational databases and is suitable for applications that require structured data storage.

Key Features of Cloud SQL:

1. **Managed Service**: Google takes care of database maintenance tasks such as backups, patching, and replication, allowing you to focus on your application.
2. **Scalability**: Cloud SQL instances can be easily scaled vertically by changing the machine type or horizontally by adding read replicas for improved performance.
3. **High Availability**: It offers automatic failover and replication for high availability, minimizing downtime.
4. **Security**: Cloud SQL provides robust security features, including data encryption, IAM integration, and private IP connectivity.
5. **Compatibility**: Supports standard SQL, making it compatible with a wide range of applications and tools.
6. **Database Engine Support**: Cloud SQL supports MySQL, PostgreSQL, and SQL Server, giving you flexibility in choosing your preferred database engine.

Cloud Spanner

CLOUD SPANNER IS A globally distributed, horizontally scalable, and strongly consistent database service. It is designed for mission-critical applications that require both high availability and strong consistency across multiple regions.

Key Features of Cloud Spanner:

1. **Global Distribution**: Cloud Spanner allows you to distribute your data across multiple regions for low-latency access and high availability.
2. **Strong Consistency**: It offers strong external consistency, making it suitable for applications with strict data

consistency requirements.

3. **Horizontal Scalability**: Cloud Spanner can automatically scale to handle increased workloads and data volumes.
4. **Automatic Sharding**: Data is automatically sharded and distributed across servers, eliminating the need for manual partitioning.
5. **SQL Support**: You can use standard SQL for querying data in Cloud Spanner, making it developer-friendly.
6. **ACID Transactions**: It supports ACID transactions, ensuring data integrity and consistency.

Choosing Between Cloud SQL and Cloud Spanner

WHEN DECIDING BETWEEN Cloud SQL and Cloud Spanner, consider the following factors:

- **Consistency Requirements**: If your application requires strong consistency across regions, Cloud Spanner is the better choice.

- **Global Distribution**: If your application needs low-latency access and high availability across the globe, Cloud Spanner's global distribution capabilities are ideal.

- **Vertical Scalability**: For applications that can benefit from vertical scalability (e.g., increasing CPU and memory), Cloud SQL is a good fit.

- **Database Engine**: Consider the database engine your application uses. Cloud SQL supports MySQL, PostgreSQL, and SQL Server, while Cloud Spanner provides its distributed SQL database.

- **Complexity**: Cloud Spanner is more complex to set up and manage due to its distributed nature. If simplicity is a priority, Cloud SQL may be preferable.

In summary, Cloud SQL is a suitable choice for traditional relational databases and applications with moderate scalability and consistency requirements. Cloud Spanner is ideal for globally distributed, highly available, and strongly consistent applications, especially when strong external consistency is crucial. The choice between the two depends on your specific use case and requirements.

4.4 Datastore and Firestore: NoSQL Solutions

GOOGLE CLOUD PLATFORM (GCP) offers two NoSQL database solutions, Datastore and Firestore, for handling non-relational data. In this section, we'll explore these services, their features, and when to use each one based on your application's requirements.

Datastore

CLOUD DATASTORE, ALSO known as Google Cloud Datastore, is a fully managed NoSQL database service designed for high availability and scalability. It provides a schema-less data model and is suitable for a wide range of use cases, including web and mobile applications.

Key Features of Datastore:

1. **Schema-less**: Datastore is schema-less, allowing you to store structured or semi-structured data without the need for predefined schemas.

2. **Automatic Scaling**: It automatically scales to handle varying workloads and data volumes.
3. **High Availability**: Datastore offers high availability and data redundancy across multiple zones.
4. **Strong Consistency**: It provides strong consistency for reads and eventual consistency for writes.
5. **Query Capabilities**: You can perform complex queries using Datastore's query language.
6. **Integration**: Datastore integrates seamlessly with other GCP services like App Engine and BigQuery.

Firestore

CLOUD FIRESTORE, ALSO known as Google Cloud Firestore, is a serverless, NoSQL document database that offers real-time data synchronization and offline support. It is designed for applications that require real-time updates and collaboration.

Key Features of Firestore:

1. **Document-based**: Firestore stores data in documents, collections, and subcollections, making it suitable for hierarchical and nested data structures.
2. **Real-time Updates**: It supports real-time data synchronization across web and mobile clients, allowing for live updates.
3. **Offline Support**: Firestore enables offline data access and automatic data synchronization when the device reconnects.
4. **Scalable**: Firestore automatically scales to handle increased load and data growth.
5. **Serverless**: You don't need to manage servers or infrastructure; Firestore is fully managed.

6. **Security**: Firestore integrates with GCP Identity and Access Management (IAM) for security and access control.

Choosing Between Datastore and Firestore

WHEN DECIDING BETWEEN Datastore and Firestore, consider the following factors:

- **Data Model**: Datastore is suitable for applications with flexible or semi-structured data, while Firestore is better for hierarchical and document-based data.

- **Real-time Updates**: If your application requires real-time updates and offline support, Firestore is the preferred choice.

- **Integration**: Datastore integrates well with GCP services like App Engine, while Firestore is designed for broader web and mobile application integration.

- **Querying**: Datastore offers more powerful querying capabilities, making it suitable for complex queries.

- **Simplicity**: Firestore's document-based model and real-time synchronization make it simpler to work with for certain use cases.

- **Strong Consistency**: Datastore provides strong consistency for reads, which may be required for specific applications.

In summary, Datastore is a versatile NoSQL database that is well-suited for various use cases with semi-structured data and complex queries. Firestore, on the other hand, is ideal for applications that require real-time updates, offline support, and hierarchical data structures. The choice between the two depends on your specific application requirements and data model.

4.5 Best Practices for Data Management in GCP

EFFICIENT DATA MANAGEMENT is essential to maximize the benefits of Google Cloud Platform (GCP) while maintaining data integrity, security, and cost-effectiveness. In this section, we'll explore best practices for managing data in GCP, ensuring that your data remains accessible, secure, and optimized for performance.

1. Data Lifecycle Management

1.1. Define Data Retention Policies: Determine how long you need to retain different types of data. Implement automated data deletion or archiving based on these policies to avoid unnecessary storage costs.

1.2. Data Classification: Classify data based on its sensitivity and regulatory requirements. Apply appropriate access controls, encryption, and auditing based on data classification.

1.3. Data Versioning: Implement version control for critical datasets to track changes over time. Google Cloud Storage provides versioning capabilities for this purpose.

2. Data Security

2.1. Encryption: Encrypt data both in transit and at rest. Use Google-managed encryption keys (Customer-Managed

Encryption Keys) or your own encryption keys for added security.

2.2. Identity and Access Management (IAM): Implement granular access controls using IAM to ensure that only authorized users and services can access your data.

2.3. Audit and Monitoring: Enable auditing and monitoring of data access and changes using Google Cloud's logging and monitoring services to detect and respond to security incidents.

3. Data Storage Optimization

3.1. Object Lifecycle Policies: Use object lifecycle policies in Google Cloud Storage to automatically delete or transition data to less expensive storage classes as it ages.

3.2. Data Compression: Compress data before storage to reduce storage costs and improve transfer speeds.

3.3. Use Appropriate Storage Classes: Select the appropriate storage class in Google Cloud Storage based on the access patterns and retrieval latency requirements of your data.

4. Data Transfer and Migration

4.1. Transfer Service: Utilize Google's transfer services for efficient data transfer into GCP, especially when migrating large volumes of data from on-premises or other cloud providers.

4.2. Dataflow for ETL: Use Google Cloud Dataflow for Extract, Transform, Load (ETL) tasks to transform and transfer data from source to target systems efficiently.

5. Data Backup and Disaster Recovery

5.1. Regular Backups: Implement regular backups of critical data to ensure data recoverability in case of data loss or disasters.

5.2. Disaster Recovery Plan: Develop and test a disaster recovery plan that includes data recovery procedures and ensures business continuity.

6. Data Governance and Compliance

6.1. Data Governance Framework: Establish a data governance framework that includes data ownership, stewardship, and compliance with data regulations (e.g., GDPR, HIPAA).

6.2. Compliance Tools: Leverage Google Cloud's compliance tools and resources to ensure that your data meets industry-specific compliance requirements.

7. Cost Optimization

7.1. Resource Cleanup: Periodically review and clean up unused or unnecessary resources to optimize costs. Use tools like Google Cloud's Cost Management tools for cost visibility.

7.2. Right-Sizing: Adjust the size and type of resources (e.g., VM instances, storage) to match your actual workload requirements, avoiding over-provisioning.

8. Data Quality and Validation

8.1. Data Validation: Implement data validation checks to ensure

data quality, consistency, and accuracy as data is ingested and processed.

8.2. Data Catalogs: Use data catalogs and metadata management tools to document and discover data assets within your organization.

BY FOLLOWING THESE best practices, you can effectively manage your data in Google Cloud Platform, ensuring that it remains secure, compliant, cost-effective, and optimized for performance. Implementing these practices will help you derive maximum value from your data while minimizing risks and operational challenges.

Chapter 5: Containers and Kubernetes in GCP

5.1 Understanding Containers and Their Importance

CONTAINERS HAVE REVOLUTIONIZED the way applications are developed, deployed, and managed in modern IT environments. In this section, we'll delve into the concept of containers, why they are essential, and how Google Cloud Platform (GCP) provides tools and services to work with containers effectively.

What Are Containers?

CONTAINERS ARE LIGHTWEIGHT, standalone, and executable packages that encapsulate an application and its dependencies, including libraries, configurations, and runtime environments. They provide a consistent and isolated environment for running applications, ensuring that they work consistently across different environments, from development to production.

Key Characteristics of Containers:

- **Isolation**: Containers run in isolated environments, which means they don't interfere with each other or the host system.

- **Portability**: Containers are highly portable and can run on any system that supports containerization, irrespective of the underlying infrastructure.

• **Efficiency**: Containers share the host OS kernel, making them lightweight and efficient in terms of resource utilization.

• **Scalability**: Containers are easily scalable, allowing you to replicate and distribute applications across multiple instances effortlessly.

Importance of Containers

CONTAINERS HAVE GAINED immense popularity for several reasons:

1. **Consistency**: Containers ensure that applications behave consistently across different environments, reducing deployment issues and "it works on my machine" problems.
2. **Isolation**: They offer application-level isolation, enhancing security and preventing conflicts between applications and dependencies.
3. **Portability**: Containers can run anywhere, from on-premises data centers to cloud environments, enabling seamless hybrid and multi-cloud deployments.
4. **DevOps and CI/CD**: Containers are an integral part of modern DevOps practices, enabling rapid development, testing, and continuous integration/continuous deployment (CI/CD) pipelines.
5. **Resource Efficiency**: Containers are resource-efficient, enabling better utilization of server resources and cost savings.

Google Cloud Platform and Containers

GCP PROVIDES A ROBUST ecosystem for working with containers, with a focus on Kubernetes as the orchestrator. Kubernetes is an open-source container orchestration platform that automates the deployment, scaling, and management of containerized applications.

Key GCP Services for Containers:

1. **Google Kubernetes Engine (GKE)**: GKE is a managed Kubernetes service that simplifies the deployment and management of Kubernetes clusters on GCP.
2. **Container Registry**: Google's container image registry allows you to store, manage, and deploy container images securely.
3. **Cloud Build**: Cloud Build offers continuous integration and delivery (CI/CD) capabilities, automating the building and testing of containerized applications.
4. **Anthos**: Google's hybrid and multi-cloud platform, Anthos, enables you to manage and deploy applications consistently across on-premises and cloud environments using Kubernetes.

IN THE FOLLOWING SECTIONS, we will explore these GCP services in more detail and learn how to leverage them for container orchestration, application deployment, and scaling.

5.2 Introduction to Kubernetes

KUBERNETES, OFTEN ABBREVIATED as K8s, is an open-source container orchestration platform that automates the deployment, scaling, and management of containerized applications.

It was originally developed by Google and is now maintained by the Cloud Native Computing Foundation (CNCF). Kubernetes provides a robust framework for container orchestration, making it easier to manage complex container-based applications in production environments.

Key Concepts in Kubernetes

BEFORE DIVING DEEPER into Kubernetes, it's essential to understand some fundamental concepts:

1. Nodes: Nodes are the underlying machines (virtual or physical) that run containers. Each node has the necessary tools and services to manage containers.

2. Pods: Pods are the smallest deployable units in Kubernetes. They can contain one or more containers that share the same network namespace and storage volumes.

3. ReplicaSets: ReplicaSets ensure that a specified number of pod replicas are running at all times. They are responsible for maintaining the desired number of pods in the cluster.

4. Services: Services provide networking and load balancing for pods. They allow applications to discover and communicate with each other within the cluster.

5. Deployments: Deployments manage the rollout and updates of applications. They enable you to specify the desired state of your application and ensure that it is maintained.

6. ConfigMaps and Secrets: ConfigMaps store configuration data as key-value pairs, while Secrets store sensitive information like

passwords and tokens securely.

7. Ingress: Ingress controllers and resources allow you to manage external access to services, typically for HTTP routing.

Key Features of Kubernetes

KUBERNETES OFFERS SEVERAL key features that make it a powerful tool for container orchestration:

1. Scalability: Kubernetes can automatically scale applications based on CPU usage, memory, or custom metrics.

2. Rolling Updates: Deployments support rolling updates, allowing you to update applications without downtime or service interruptions.

3. Self-Healing: Kubernetes monitors the health of containers and restarts them if they fail, ensuring high availability.

4. Load Balancing: Services provide built-in load balancing for applications, distributing traffic to healthy pods.

5. Rolling Rollbacks: In case of issues with an update, Kubernetes supports rolling back to the previous version of the application.

6. Resource Management: Kubernetes allows you to allocate and manage resources like CPU and memory for containers.

GCP and Kubernetes

GOOGLE CLOUD PLATFORM (GCP) offers Google Kubernetes Engine (GKE), a managed Kubernetes service that simplifies the deployment and management of Kubernetes clusters. With GKE, you can take advantage of Google's infrastructure and expertise in running Kubernetes at scale.

Key GKE Features:

1. **Managed Control Plane**: GKE manages the control plane, ensuring high availability and automatic upgrades.
2. **Integration with GCP Services**: GKE seamlessly integrates with other GCP services, such as Cloud Load Balancing, Cloud Monitoring, and Cloud Logging.
3. **Node Pools**: GKE allows you to create node pools with different machine types, enabling you to optimize resources for different workloads.
4. **Autoscaling**: GKE supports autoscaling of node pools to handle varying workloads.
5. **Private Cluster**: You can create private GKE clusters with no external IP addresses for enhanced security.
6. **Node Auto-Repair**: GKE automatically repairs nodes that experience issues, improving cluster reliability.

IN THE FOLLOWING SECTIONS, we'll explore how to create and manage Kubernetes clusters using Google Kubernetes Engine (GKE) and deploy containerized applications on the platform. Understanding Kubernetes is crucial for effectively utilizing containerization and orchestration in the cloud.

5.3 Deploying Kubernetes Clusters with GKE (Google Kubernetes Engine)

GOOGLE KUBERNETES ENGINE (GKE) is a fully managed Kubernetes service provided by Google Cloud Platform (GCP). It simplifies the process of creating, managing, and scaling Kubernetes clusters, allowing you to focus on deploying and running containerized applications. In this section, we will explore how to deploy Kubernetes clusters using GKE.

Prerequisites

BEFORE YOU BEGIN, ENSURE that you have the following prerequisites:

1. **Google Cloud Platform Account**: You need a GCP account to use GKE. If you don't have one, you can sign up for a free trial.
2. **Google Cloud SDK**: Install the Google Cloud SDK on your local machine to interact with GKE from the command line.

Steps to Deploy a GKE Cluster

FOLLOW THESE STEPS to deploy a Kubernetes cluster using GKE:

1. Enable the GKE API

BEFORE CREATING A CLUSTER, ensure that the Google Kubernetes Engine API is enabled in your GCP project. You can enable it using the GCP Console or the Google Cloud SDK with the following command:

```
gcloud services enable container.googleapis.com
```

2. Set Up Authentication

AUTHENTICATE WITH YOUR GCP account by running the following command and following the instructions to log in:

gcloud auth login

3. Create a GKE Cluster

USE THE gcloud container clusters create command to create a GKE cluster. Specify the cluster name, zone, number of nodes, and machine type, as shown below:

gcloud container clusters create my-cluster \

—zone us-central1-a \

—num-nodes 3 \

—machine-type n1-standard-2

This command creates a cluster named my-cluster with 3 nodes in the us-central1-a zone, using the n1-standard-2 machine type. Adjust these parameters to match your requirements.

4. Configure kubectl

TO INTERACT WITH YOUR GKE cluster, you need to configure kubectl, the Kubernetes command-line tool, to use the cluster's credentials. Run the following command to do so:

gcloud container clusters get-credentials my-cluster—zone us-central1-a

Replace my-cluster and us-central1-a with your cluster's name and zone.

5. Verify the Cluster

YOU CAN VERIFY THAT your cluster is running and healthy by running the following command:

kubectl get nodes

You should see a list of nodes in your cluster.

6. Deploy Applications

WITH YOUR GKE CLUSTER set up, you can now deploy containerized applications using Kubernetes manifests (YAML files) or Helm charts.

Cluster Management with GKE

GKE PROVIDES SEVERAL features for cluster management:

- **Node Pools**: You can create node pools with different machine types and configurations to optimize resources for different workloads.
- **Autoscaling**: GKE supports node autoscaling, automatically adjusting the number of nodes based on resource utilization.
- **Automatic Updates**: GKE can automatically update the cluster's nodes to ensure security and stability.

- **Node Auto-Repair**: Nodes that experience issues are automatically repaired by GKE to maintain cluster reliability.

GKE simplifies the management of Kubernetes clusters, making it easier to deploy and run containerized applications in a production-ready environment. It also integrates seamlessly with other GCP services, enhancing your cloud-native application stack.

5.4 Container Registry and Artifact Repository

CONTAINER REGISTRY is a managed Docker container image registry provided by Google Cloud Platform (GCP). It allows you to store, manage, and deploy Docker container images securely. Artifact Repository is another GCP service that provides a repository for storing and managing various artifact types, including container images. In this section, we will explore both Container Registry and Artifact Repository.

Google Container Registry

GOOGLE CONTAINER REGISTRY is designed specifically for Docker container images and integrates seamlessly with other GCP services like Google Kubernetes Engine (GKE) and Cloud Build. Here are some key features of Google Container Registry:

1. Secure Storage: Container Registry provides secure storage for your container images with fine-grained access control using Google Cloud Identity and Access Management (IAM).

2. Regional and Multi-Regional Storage: You can choose the storage location that best suits your needs, whether regional or

multi-regional, for redundancy and low-latency access.

3. Integration with CI/CD: Container Registry integrates with Cloud Build for continuous integration and delivery (CI/CD) workflows, making it easy to build, test, and deploy container images.

4. Versioning and Tagging: You can version and tag container images, allowing you to manage different versions of your application.

5. Easy Deployment: Container images stored in Container Registry can be easily deployed to Google Kubernetes Engine or other container orchestration platforms.

HERE'S A BASIC EXAMPLE of pushing a Docker image to Google Container Registry:

```
# Build a Docker image

docker build -t gcr.io/my-project/my-app:v1 .

# Authenticate with GCP

gcloud auth configure-docker

# Push the image to Container Registry

docker push gcr.io/my-project/my-app:v1
```

Google Artifact Registry

GOOGLE ARTIFACT REGISTRY is a multi-format artifact repository that supports container images, Docker images, Maven, npm, and more. It is designed to store and manage various types of software artifacts. Here are some key features of Google Artifact Registry:

1. Artifact Types: Artifact Registry supports various artifact types, making it a versatile repository for different software components and libraries.

2. Versioning: Similar to Container Registry, Artifact Registry allows you to version artifacts, enabling you to manage different versions of your software.

3. Fine-Grained Access Control: Artifact Registry provides IAM-based access control to restrict who can access and modify artifacts.

4. Integration with CI/CD: You can easily integrate Artifact Registry into your CI/CD pipelines for artifact management.

5. Container Image Vulnerability Scanning: Artifact Registry offers vulnerability scanning for container images, helping you identify and address security issues.

HERE'S A BASIC EXAMPLE of pushing a Docker image to Google Artifact Registry:

 # Build a Docker image

docker build -t us-central1-docker.pkg.dev/my-project/my-repo/my-app:v1 .

 # Authenticate with GCP

gcloud auth configure-docker us-central1-docker.pkg.dev

 # Push the image to Artifact Registry

docker push us-central1-docker.pkg.dev/my-project/my-repo/my-app:v1

Choosing Between Container Registry and Artifact Registry

THE CHOICE BETWEEN Container Registry and Artifact Registry depends on your specific requirements. If you primarily work with Docker container images, Container Registry is a dedicated and optimized solution for Docker images. However, if you need a versatile repository that supports various artifact types, including Docker images, and provides advanced features like vulnerability scanning, Artifact Registry is a suitable choice.

Both Container Registry and Artifact Registry offer secure and scalable options for artifact management, making them valuable components of a CI/CD pipeline in Google Cloud Platform.

5.5 Managing and Scaling Containers in GCP

GOOGLE CLOUD PLATFORM (GCP) provides a range of tools and services for managing and scaling containers effectively. In this section, we'll explore the key aspects of managing and scaling containers in GCP.

1. Google Kubernetes Engine (GKE): GKE is a managed Kubernetes service that simplifies container orchestration. It allows you to create, deploy, and manage containerized applications with ease. GKE offers features such as automatic scaling, automatic node upgrades, and node auto-repair to ensure the availability and reliability of your container workloads.**

HERE'S A BASIC EXAMPLE of scaling a GKE cluster manually using the gcloud command:

 # Resize the node pool to add more nodes

gcloud container clusters resize my-cluster—node-pool default-pool—num-nodes 5—zone us-central1-a

2. Horizontal Pod Autoscaling (HPA): In Kubernetes, you can configure Horizontal Pod Autoscaling (HPA) to automatically adjust the number of pod replicas based on resource utilization metrics such as CPU or memory usage. GKE supports HPA, allowing your application to scale dynamically in response to changing workloads.**

HERE'S AN EXAMPLE OF creating an HPA in Kubernetes:

apiVersion: autoscaling/v2beta2

kind: HorizontalPodAutoscaler

metadata:

name: my-app-hpa

spec:

```
scaleTargetRef:
apiVersion: apps/v1
kind: Deployment
name: my-app-deployment
minReplicas: 1
maxReplicas: 10
metrics:
- type: Resource
resource:
name: cpu
targetAverageUtilization: 80
```

3. Stackdriver Kubernetes Monitoring: Stackdriver is a GCP service that provides comprehensive monitoring and logging for containerized applications. It allows you to gain insights into the performance and health of your containers, clusters, and workloads. You can set up alerts, create custom dashboards, and troubleshoot issues effectively.**

4. Cloud Logging and Cloud Monitoring: GCP offers Cloud Logging and Cloud Monitoring, which are integrated with GKE. Cloud Logging allows you to collect, view, and analyze logs generated by your containers and applications. Cloud Monitoring enables you to set up custom metrics, create alerts, and monitor the performance of your containerized**

workloads.

5. Node Pools: GKE allows you to create multiple node pools within a cluster, each with its own configuration and characteristics. Node pools can be used to optimize resource allocation for different workloads. For example, you can create a node pool with high CPU resources for CPU-intensive tasks and another with high memory resources for memory-intensive tasks.**

6. Auto-Scaling: GKE supports automatic node scaling based on the utilization of node resources. You can configure auto-scaling policies to ensure that your cluster adapts to varying workloads, adding or removing nodes as needed.**

HERE'S AN EXAMPLE OF configuring auto-scaling for a node pool in GKE:

 # Enable auto-scaling for a node pool

gcloud container node-pools update my-node-pool—cluster my-cluster—enable-autoscaling—min-nodes 1—max-nodes 10

7. Custom Metrics: GKE allows you to define custom metrics and thresholds for auto-scaling your workloads. This gives you the flexibility to scale based on application-specific metrics and requirements.**

8. Cluster Management: GCP provides various tools and features for managing clusters efficiently. You can upgrade the Kubernetes version of your clusters, enable automatic security patching, and perform rolling updates to keep your clusters up to date and secure.**

MANAGING AND SCALING containers effectively is crucial for optimizing resource usage and ensuring high availability and performance of your applications. GCP's suite of container management services and tools provides the necessary capabilities to achieve these goals and meet the demands of modern, containerized workloads.

Chapter 6: Developing and Deploying Applications

6.1 Building Applications in the Cloud

BUILDING APPLICATIONS in the cloud offers numerous advantages, including scalability, flexibility, and accessibility. Google Cloud Platform (GCP) provides a robust environment for developing and deploying cloud-native applications. In this section, we will explore the key concepts and practices for building cloud-based applications in GCP.

Cloud-Native Application Development

CLOUD-NATIVE APPLICATION development is an approach that leverages cloud resources and services to create applications that are highly scalable, resilient, and agile. Key characteristics of cloud-native applications include:

- **Microservices Architecture**: Cloud-native applications are often built using microservices, where each component of the application is a separate, independently deployable service. This architecture promotes flexibility and scalability.

- **Containerization**: Containers, such as Docker, are commonly used to package and deploy application components. They provide consistency in development and production environments.

- **Orchestration**: Container orchestration platforms like Kubernetes are used to manage and scale containerized applications. Kubernetes simplifies deployment, scaling, and management of application containers.

- **Serverless Computing**: Serverless platforms, like Cloud Functions and App Engine, allow developers to focus on code without worrying about infrastructure management. These platforms automatically scale based on demand.

Choosing the Right Compute Service

GCP OFFERS A RANGE of compute services, and selecting the appropriate one for your application is essential. Consider the following options:

- **Compute Engine**: Use Compute Engine for virtual machine-based workloads that require complete control over the underlying infrastructure. You can choose machine types and customize VM instances to meet specific requirements.

- **Kubernetes Engine (GKE)**: GKE is ideal for containerized applications. It manages the Kubernetes cluster, making it easier to deploy, scale, and manage container workloads.

- **App Engine**: App Engine is a fully managed platform for building and deploying web applications. It abstracts away infrastructure management, allowing developers to focus solely on code.

- **Cloud Functions**: For event-driven, serverless computing, Cloud Functions are suitable. They automatically scale in response to events and are charged based on usage.

Continuous Integration and Continuous Deployment (CI/CD)

IMPLEMENTING CI/CD pipelines is crucial for efficient development and deployment in the cloud. Tools like Cloud Build enable automation of build and deployment processes. A typical CI/CD pipeline includes stages for code building, testing, and deployment to various environments, such as development, staging, and production.

Here's a simplified example of a CI/CD pipeline configuration in Cloud Build:

```
steps:

- name: 'gcr.io/cloud-builders/npm'

args: ['install']

- name: 'gcr.io/cloud-builders/npm'

args: ['test']

- name: 'gcr.io/cloud-builders/gcloud'

args: ['app', 'deploy']
```

Serverless Solutions

GCP PROVIDES SERVERLESS options like Cloud Functions and App Engine for specific use cases. Cloud Functions allow you to run single-purpose, event-driven functions without managing servers. App Engine abstracts infrastructure management, offering a platform for building scalable web applications.

Here's a basic example of creating a Cloud Function in GCP:

```
exports.myFunction = (req, res) => {

res.status(200).send('Hello, Cloud Function!');

};
```

Monitoring and Logging

MONITORING AND LOGGING are critical aspects of cloud application development. Stackdriver Monitoring and Stackdriver Logging in GCP provide tools to monitor application performance, collect metrics, and analyze logs. Setting up alerts and creating custom dashboards helps you proactively identify and address issues.

In conclusion, building cloud-native applications in GCP involves adopting modern development practices, choosing the right compute service, implementing CI/CD pipelines, leveraging serverless solutions, and monitoring application health. GCP's robust ecosystem of services and tools empowers developers to create scalable and resilient cloud applications.

6.2 Choosing the Right Computing Service for Your Application

SELECTING THE APPROPRIATE computing service for your application is a crucial decision in the cloud-native development process. Google Cloud Platform (GCP) offers a variety of computing services to cater to different use cases and requirements. In this section, we will explore the factors to consider when choosing the right computing service for your application.

Compute Engine

GOOGLE COMPUTE ENGINE provides virtual machines (VMs) on which you can run your applications. It offers a high level of control over the underlying infrastructure, allowing you to choose machine types, customize VM instances, and install software as needed. Compute Engine is suitable for:

- **Legacy Applications**: If you have existing applications that are not containerized or require a specific OS environment, Compute Engine may be the right choice.

- **High Performance**: For workloads that demand high compute and memory resources, Compute Engine provides customizable VMs with options for GPUs and high-memory instances.

- **Control and Flexibility**: If you need complete control over the VMs, including managing operating systems and software, Compute Engine offers the flexibility to do so.

Kubernetes Engine (GKE)

GOOGLE KUBERNETES ENGINE is a managed Kubernetes service that simplifies the deployment, scaling, and management of containerized applications. It is ideal for applications built using a microservices architecture and containers. GKE is suitable for:

- **Containerized Applications**: If your application is designed using containers, GKE provides a managed Kubernetes environment for orchestrating and scaling containers.

- **Scalability**: GKE automates the scaling of containerized workloads based on demand, making it suitable for applications with varying traffic loads.

- **Orchestration**: If you need container orchestration features like rolling updates, load balancing, and self-healing, GKE simplifies these tasks.

App Engine

GOOGLE APP ENGINE IS a fully managed platform for building and deploying web applications and APIs. It abstracts away infrastructure management, allowing developers to focus solely on writing code. App Engine is suitable for:

- **Web Applications**: If your application is a web-based service, App Engine simplifies deployment and scaling without the need to manage virtual machines.

- **Serverless**: App Engine is considered a serverless platform, as it automatically handles scaling based on incoming traffic and offers a pay-as-you-go pricing model.

- **Rapid Development**: If you want to quickly develop and deploy applications without worrying about infrastructure details, App Engine offers a streamlined development process.

Cloud Functions

GOOGLE CLOUD FUNCTIONS is a serverless compute service that allows you to run single-purpose, event-driven functions without managing servers. It is suitable for event-driven, lightweight workloads. Cloud Functions are ideal for:

- **Event-Driven Workflows**: If your application needs to respond to events from various sources, such as HTTP requests, Cloud Pub/Sub messages, or changes in Cloud Storage, Cloud Functions is a good choice.

- **Cost Efficiency**: Cloud Functions charge you only for the compute resources used during execution, making it cost-effective for sporadic or low-traffic workloads.

- **Simplified Development**: Developers can focus on writing code for specific functions without dealing with server provisioning or management.

Hybrid Approaches

IN SOME CASES, A HYBRID approach using multiple computing services may be appropriate. For example, you can use Compute Engine for certain backend processes while employing App Engine or Cloud Functions for frontend or event-driven components. GCP provides the flexibility to mix and match services based on your application's needs.

When choosing a computing service for your application, it's essential to consider factors such as application architecture, scalability requirements, cost constraints, and developer preferences. GCP's range of compute services ensures that you can find the right fit for your specific use case, allowing you to build and deploy cloud-native applications effectively.

6.3 Continuous Integration and Deployment with Cloud Build

CONTINUOUS INTEGRATION and Continuous Deployment (CI/CD) are essential practices in modern application development, especially when working with cloud-native applications in Google Cloud Platform (GCP). Google Cloud Build is a fully managed CI/CD platform that helps automate the build, test, and deployment processes. In this section, we will explore the key concepts and practices of CI/CD with Cloud Build.

Benefits of CI/CD

CI/CD IS A SOFTWARE engineering practice that aims to enhance the development workflow by automating various stages of the application lifecycle. It offers several benefits, including:

- **Faster Development**: CI/CD streamlines the development process by automating tasks, reducing manual errors, and enabling quicker iterations.

- **Consistency**: Automated builds and deployments ensure consistency across development, testing, and production environments.

- **Quality Assurance**: Automated testing helps catch bugs and issues early in the development cycle, improving the overall quality of the application.

- **Efficient Collaboration**: CI/CD facilitates collaboration among development teams by providing a standardized way to build, test, and deploy code.

Setting Up CI/CD with Cloud Build

TO SET UP CI/CD WITH Cloud Build, you'll need the following components:

1. **Source Code Repository**: Your application code should

be stored in a version control system like Git, hosted on platforms like Cloud Source Repositories, GitHub, or Bitbucket.

2. **Build Configuration**: You define a build configuration file (e.g., cloudbuild.yaml) that specifies how Cloud Build should build and package your application. Here's a simplified example:

```
steps:

- name: 'gcr.io/cloud-builders/npm'

args: ['install']

- name: 'gcr.io/cloud-builders/npm'

args: ['test']

- name: 'gcr.io/cloud-builders/gcloud'

args: ['app', 'deploy']
```

1. **Triggers**: You create triggers that specify when Cloud Build should automatically initiate builds. Triggers can be set up to build and deploy code changes pushed to specific branches, tags, or in response to events.

CI/CD Pipeline Stages

A TYPICAL CI/CD PIPELINE consists of several stages:

1. **Code Build**: Cloud Build fetches the source code from the repository, builds the application, and packages it.
2. **Testing**: Automated tests are executed to ensure the application functions correctly and meets quality standards.

3. **Artifact Storage**: Built artifacts are stored in a secure location for deployment. Google Cloud Storage is commonly used for this purpose.
4. **Deployment**: The application is deployed to the target environment, which can be a development, staging, or production environment.
5. **Monitoring and Validation**: Post-deployment monitoring and validation ensure that the application behaves as expected in the production environment.

Cloud Build Workflow

HERE'S AN OVERVIEW of the typical workflow when using Cloud Build for CI/CD:

1. Developers push code changes to the version control repository.
2. A trigger configured in Cloud Build detects the code changes and starts a new build.
3. Cloud Build follows the build configuration instructions, including building, testing, and packaging the application.
4. If the tests pass, Cloud Build deploys the application to the specified environment.
5. Monitoring and validation tools are used to verify the deployed application's performance and functionality.
6. If everything is successful, the changes are promoted to production.

Best Practices for CI/CD with Cloud Build

TO MAKE THE MOST OF CI/CD with Cloud Build, consider the following best practices:

- Automate as much as possible: Automate the build, test, and deployment processes to minimize manual intervention.

- Implement thorough testing: Ensure comprehensive automated testing to catch issues early in the development cycle.

- Use version control effectively: Maintain a clear version control strategy and use branching for feature development and bug fixes.

- Secure your pipeline: Protect your CI/CD pipeline from unauthorized access and use encryption for sensitive data.

- Monitor and log: Implement monitoring and logging for your CI/CD pipeline to detect and address any issues promptly.

- Promote changes cautiously: Use a clear promotion process for moving changes from development to production to avoid unintended consequences.

CI/CD with Cloud Build empowers development teams to accelerate the software development lifecycle while maintaining high-quality standards. By automating repetitive tasks and providing a structured workflow, Cloud Build simplifies the process of building and deploying cloud-native applications in GCP.

6.4 Serverless Solutions: Cloud Functions and App Engine

SERVERLESS COMPUTING has gained immense popularity in recent years due to its simplicity and cost-effectiveness. Google Cloud Platform (GCP) offers two prominent serverless solutions: Google Cloud Functions and Google App Engine. In this section, we will explore both options and discuss when to use each.

Google Cloud Functions

GOOGLE CLOUD FUNCTIONS is a serverless compute service that allows developers to run single-purpose, event-driven functions without the need to manage servers. Key features of Cloud Functions include:

- **Event-Driven Execution**: Cloud Functions are triggered by events, such as HTTP requests, Cloud Pub/Sub messages, or changes in Cloud Storage. This event-driven model is suitable for various use cases, including data processing, automation, and real-time processing.

- **Pay-as-You-Go Pricing**: Cloud Functions offer a cost-effective pricing model where you pay only for the compute resources used during function execution. There is no need to provision or manage servers, reducing operational overhead.

- **Automatic Scaling**: Cloud Functions automatically scale based on incoming traffic or events. Whether you have a few requests per day or millions per minute, the service handles the scaling for you.

- **Simplified Development**: Developers can focus solely on writing code for specific functions, without worrying about infrastructure provisioning, scaling, or maintenance.

Use Cases for Cloud Functions:

- Real-time data processing and analysis.
- Automation of repetitive tasks.
- Building serverless APIs and webhooks.
- Handling asynchronous events in microservices architectures.

Google App Engine

GOOGLE APP ENGINE IS a fully managed platform-as-a-service (PaaS) that simplifies application deployment and scaling. Key features of App Engine include:

- **Managed Infrastructure**: App Engine abstracts away the underlying infrastructure, allowing developers to focus solely on writing code. Google manages the servers, operating systems, and runtime environments.
- **Automatic Scaling**: Similar to Cloud Functions, App Engine automatically scales your application based on incoming traffic. It can handle bursts of traffic or gradual increases without manual intervention.
- **Built-in Services**: App Engine provides built-in services for data storage, caching, authentication, and more. These

services help developers accelerate application development by using managed components.

- **Support for Multiple Runtimes**: App Engine supports various programming languages and runtimes, including Python, Java, Node.js, and more. Developers can choose the runtime that best suits their application.

Use Cases for App Engine:

- Web applications and APIs.
- Backend services for mobile apps.
- Content management systems (CMS).
- Microservices with HTTP-based communication.

Choosing Between Cloud Functions and App Engine

CHOOSING BETWEEN CLOUD Functions and App Engine depends on your application's requirements:

- Use Cloud Functions when you have specific, event-driven tasks or need to execute code in response to events. It's ideal for small, focused functions.

- Use App Engine when you want to build and deploy web applications, APIs, or backend services. App Engine provides a more traditional development experience with the flexibility to choose your programming language and runtime.

In some cases, you might even use both services within the same application to benefit from the strengths of each. For example, you can use Cloud Functions to handle asynchronous tasks triggered by events and App Engine to serve your web application's frontend.

Ultimately, the choice between Cloud Functions and App Engine should align with your application's architecture, development team's skills, and specific use cases. GCP offers the flexibility to use the right serverless solution for the right job, allowing you to build scalable and cost-effective applications.

6.5 Monitoring and Logging with Operations Suite

MONITORING AND LOGGING are critical aspects of managing applications in the cloud. Google Cloud Platform (GCP) offers Operations Suite (formerly known as Stackdriver) to help you gain insights into the performance, health, and behavior of your applications. In this section, we'll explore the capabilities of Operations Suite for monitoring and logging in GCP.

Key Components of Operations Suite

OPERATIONS SUITE COMPRISES several key components that work together to provide comprehensive monitoring and logging:

1. **Monitoring**: Google Cloud Monitoring allows you to collect and visualize metrics, set up alerts, and gain real-time insights into the health and performance of your resources. Key features include:

– **Custom Metrics**: You can create custom metrics to track specific aspects of your application's performance or business metrics.

– **Alerting Policies**: Set up alerting policies to receive notifications when predefined conditions are met, helping you proactively address issues.

– **Dashboards**: Create custom dashboards to visualize the metrics that matter most to your application's operation.

– **Integration**: Google Cloud Monitoring integrates seamlessly with various GCP services, allowing you to monitor resources such as Compute Engine, App Engine, and Kubernetes Engine.

1. **Logging**: Google Cloud Logging allows you to collect and analyze logs generated by your applications and infrastructure. Key features include:

– **Structured Logging**: Logs can be structured and include metadata, making it easier to search and analyze log entries.

– **Log-Based Metrics**: Create metrics from log data to monitor specific events or conditions within your application.

– **Advanced Filters**: Use advanced filtering and querying capabilities to find specific log entries quickly.

– **Export and Storage**: Export logs to Google Cloud Storage, BigQuery, or other destinations for long-term storage and analysis.

1. **Error Reporting**: Google Cloud Error Reporting automatically detects and aggregates errors in your applications, providing actionable insights into code issues

and exceptions.

2. **Trace**: Google Cloud Trace helps you understand the latency and performance bottlenecks in your applications by providing distributed tracing capabilities.

Monitoring Your Resources

GOOGLE CLOUD MONITORING allows you to monitor various resources and services within your GCP projects. You can set up monitoring for:

- Virtual Machines (Compute Engine)
- Containers (Kubernetes Engine, Docker)
- Serverless Functions (Cloud Functions, App Engine)
- Databases (Cloud SQL, Firestore)
- Network Services (Load Balancers, VPNs)
- And more...

You can create custom dashboards to visualize the metrics that are most relevant to your application's performance and health. By setting up alerting policies, you can receive notifications via email, SMS, or other channels when critical thresholds are exceeded.

Centralized Logging and Analysis

GOOGLE CLOUD LOGGING offers centralized logging capabilities, allowing you to collect logs from various sources, including GCP services and custom applications. Logs can be searched, filtered, and analyzed in real-time, making it easier to troubleshoot issues and gain insights into your application's behavior.

You can also create log-based metrics to monitor specific events or conditions within your logs. This helps you proactively detect issues and respond quickly to them.

Error Reporting and Tracing

GOOGLE CLOUD ERROR Reporting automatically detects and aggregates errors in your applications, providing a clear view of code issues and exceptions. This feature is particularly useful for identifying and resolving application errors in a timely manner.

Google Cloud Trace helps you gain insights into the latency and performance of your applications. By tracing requests as they traverse different components of your application, you can pinpoint performance bottlenecks and optimize your code for better responsiveness.

Integrating with Other GCP Services

OPERATIONS SUITE INTEGRATES seamlessly with other GCP services, creating a holistic monitoring and logging solution. You can link your GCP resources to Operations Suite to collect metrics and logs, making it a centralized hub for managing the observability of your entire application stack.

In summary, Operations Suite provides a comprehensive set of tools for monitoring, logging, error reporting, and tracing in Google Cloud Platform. Leveraging these capabilities, you can ensure the performance, availability, and reliability of your cloud-native applications while quickly diagnosing and resolving issues when they arise.

Chapter 7: AI and Machine Learning Services

7.1 AI and Machine Learning in the Cloud: An Overview

ARTIFICIAL INTELLIGENCE (AI) and Machine Learning (ML) have emerged as transformative technologies that enable businesses to extract valuable insights from data, automate processes, and make intelligent decisions. Google Cloud Platform (GCP) offers a comprehensive suite of AI and ML services, making it easier for developers and data scientists to harness the power of AI in their applications. In this section, we'll provide an overview of AI and ML in the cloud and explore the key AI and ML offerings within GCP.

The Role of AI and ML in Modern Applications

AI AND ML ARE INTEGRAL components of modern applications across various industries. They empower organizations to:

- **Enhance User Experiences**: AI-driven recommendations, chatbots, and personalization provide users with tailored experiences, increasing engagement and satisfaction.

- **Automate Tasks**: ML models can automate repetitive tasks, such as data entry, content moderation, and customer support, freeing up human resources for more complex tasks.

- **Predict Outcomes**: ML algorithms can analyze historical data to make predictions and forecasts, aiding decision-making in areas like finance, healthcare, and logistics.

• **Improve Efficiency**: AI can optimize processes and resource allocation, reducing operational costs and improving overall efficiency.

• **Gain Insights**: ML models uncover hidden patterns and insights in large datasets, helping businesses make data-driven decisions and discover new opportunities.

Google Cloud AI and ML Services

GCP OFFERS A WIDE RANGE of AI and ML services that cater to different needs and skill levels. Here are some of the key offerings:

1. **AI Platform**: Google's AI Platform provides a managed environment for building, training, and deploying ML models. It supports popular ML frameworks like TensorFlow and scikit-learn, making it easy for data scientists and developers to create custom models.
2. **Machine Learning APIs**: GCP offers pre-trained ML models through APIs, including Vision AI, Natural Language AI, and Translation AI. These APIs allow developers to integrate AI capabilities into their applications without extensive ML expertise.
3. **AutoML**: Google's AutoML suite enables users to build custom ML models with minimal effort. AutoML Vision, AutoML Natural Language, and AutoML Tables are examples of services that simplify the model-building process.
4. **TensorFlow**: TensorFlow, an open-source ML framework developed by Google, is widely used for building deep

learning models. GCP provides TensorFlow support and infrastructure for scalable training and deployment.

5. **BigQuery ML**: BigQuery ML allows data analysts and data scientists to create ML models directly within BigQuery, using SQL-like syntax. This simplifies the process of applying ML to large datasets.

Use Cases for GCP AI and ML Services

GCP'S AI AND ML SERVICES are applicable across various industries and use cases:

- **Image and Video Analysis**: Vision AI can be used for image recognition, content moderation, and object detection in applications like e-commerce and media.

- **Natural Language Processing (NLP)**: Natural Language AI enables sentiment analysis, language translation, and chatbot development for improved customer support and communication.

- **Predictive Analytics**: ML models can predict customer behavior, demand forecasting, and equipment maintenance, benefiting industries such as retail, manufacturing, and finance.

- **Recommendation Systems**: AI-driven recommendation engines enhance user engagement and drive revenue for e-commerce platforms, streaming services, and more.

- **Anomaly Detection**: ML can identify unusual patterns in data for fraud detection, network security, and quality control.

In summary, AI and ML have become essential tools for organizations looking to gain a competitive edge, optimize operations, and deliver exceptional user experiences. Google Cloud Platform offers a diverse set of AI and ML services that cater to different skill levels and use cases, enabling businesses to leverage the power of AI in their applications and solutions.

7.2 Introduction to AI Platform and Machine Learning APIs

GOOGLE CLOUD PLATFORM (GCP) offers a robust suite of AI and Machine Learning (ML) services that empower developers and data scientists to integrate AI capabilities into their applications. In this section, we'll delve into AI Platform and Machine Learning APIs, highlighting their key features and how they can be leveraged for various AI and ML tasks.

AI Platform: Building Custom ML Models

Overview

AI PLATFORM IS A MANAGED service that facilitates the development, training, and deployment of custom ML models. It provides a collaborative environment for data scientists and developers, making it easier to build and iterate on ML solutions. Here are some of the core features of AI Platform:

- **Scalable Training**: AI Platform allows you to train ML models at scale using Google's infrastructure. You can leverage distributed training to speed up the training process.

- **Model Versioning**: You can keep track of different versions of your ML models, making it easy to compare and roll back to previous iterations.

- **Hyperparameter Tuning**: AI Platform offers hyperparameter tuning to automatically optimize model performance by searching for the best set of hyperparameters.

- **Online Prediction**: Once your model is trained, AI Platform provides a RESTful API for online prediction, allowing real-time inference on new data.

Use Cases

AI PLATFORM IS SUITABLE for a wide range of ML use cases, including:

- **Image and Video Classification**: You can build models for image classification, object detection, and video analysis using AI Platform.

- **Natural Language Processing (NLP)**: AI Platform supports NLP tasks such as sentiment analysis, text classification, and language translation.

- **Time Series Forecasting**: For applications like demand forecasting, AI Platform can be used to build time series prediction models.

- **Recommendation Systems**: You can develop recommendation engines that personalize content or product recommendations for users.

- **Anomaly Detection**: AI Platform can help identify anomalies in data streams for fraud detection or quality control.

Machine Learning APIs: Pre-trained Models for Easy Integration

Overview

GOOGLE CLOUD OFFERS a set of pre-trained Machine Learning APIs that provide out-of-the-box AI capabilities. These APIs are designed for easy integration into applications, even if you have limited ML expertise. Here are some of the key Machine Learning APIs:

- **Vision AI**: Vision AI allows you to analyze images and videos, performing tasks like image labeling, face recognition, and content moderation.

- **Natural Language AI**: This API enables natural language processing tasks such as sentiment analysis, entity recognition, and language translation.

- **Translation AI**: With Translation AI, you can translate text between languages, making your application accessible to a global audience.

- **Video AI**: Video AI provides video analysis capabilities, including shot change detection, object tracking, and speech transcription.

- **Speech AI**: Speech AI allows for speech-to-text and text-to-speech conversion, making it valuable for applications involving voice interactions.

Use Cases

MACHINE LEARNING APIS are suitable for scenarios where you need quick and efficient AI capabilities without the need to train custom models. Use cases include:

- **Image and Video Analysis**: Vision AI is ideal for applications involving image or video content, such as social media moderation, visual search, or security surveillance.

- **Language Processing**: Natural Language AI can enhance customer support by analyzing user feedback sentiment or automate language translation in content management systems.

- **Multilingual Support**: Translation AI helps businesses expand their reach by providing multilingual content on websites and in applications.

- **Accessibility**: Text-to-speech and speech-to-text features of Speech AI improve accessibility in applications for individuals with disabilities.

In conclusion, AI Platform and Machine Learning APIs within Google Cloud Platform offer a versatile range of tools for integrating AI and ML capabilities into applications. AI Platform is suitable for building custom ML models with scalability and hyperparameter tuning, while Machine Learning APIs provide pre-trained models for quick and easy integration into various use cases, enhancing the functionality of your applications.

7.3 Building Machine Learning Models with

TensorFlow

TENSORFLOW IS AN OPEN-source machine learning framework developed by the Google Brain team. It's widely used for building and training machine learning models, including deep learning models. In this section, we'll explore TensorFlow and how it can be used to create and train machine learning models in the Google Cloud Platform (GCP) environment.

TensorFlow Overview

TENSORFLOW PROVIDES a flexible and scalable platform for developing ML models. It offers a wide range of tools and libraries for tasks such as neural networks, natural language processing, image recognition, and more. Some key features of TensorFlow include:

- **High-Level APIs**: TensorFlow offers high-level APIs like Keras, which simplifies the process of building and training neural networks.
- **TensorBoard**: A visualization toolkit that allows you to monitor and analyze model training and performance.
- **TensorFlow Extended (TFX)**: An end-to-end ML platform that includes components for data validation, feature engineering, model training, and serving.
- **TensorFlow Serving**: A system for serving machine learning models in production environments.

Using TensorFlow in GCP

GCP PROVIDES A VARIETY of services and tools for integrating TensorFlow into your machine learning workflow:

- **AI Platform**: You can use AI Platform to train and deploy TensorFlow models at scale. It supports distributed training and provides GPU and TPU (Tensor Processing Unit) support for accelerated training.

- **AI Platform Notebooks**: AI Platform Notebooks offers a managed Jupyter Notebook environment with pre-installed TensorFlow and other ML libraries, making it easy to experiment and develop models.

- **BigQuery ML**: BigQuery ML allows you to train machine learning models directly within BigQuery using SQL queries. While it doesn't replace TensorFlow for complex tasks, it's a convenient option for certain use cases.

Example: Building a TensorFlow Model in GCP

HERE'S A SIMPLIFIED example of how you can build a TensorFlow model in GCP using AI Platform Notebooks:

1. Create a Jupyter Notebook instance in AI Platform Notebooks.
2. Import TensorFlow and other necessary libraries.
3. Load your dataset from Google Cloud Storage or BigQuery.
4. Preprocess and prepare your data.
5. Build a neural network model using TensorFlow's Keras API.
6. Compile the model by specifying loss functions and optimization algorithms.
7. Train the model using your data.
8. Evaluate the model's performance using validation data.

9. Deploy the trained model on AI Platform for predictions.
10. Monitor and manage your model's performance using TensorBoard and AI Platform's tools.

TensorFlow's flexibility and integration with GCP services make it a powerful choice for machine learning tasks, from image recognition to natural language processing. Whether you're a data scientist or a developer, TensorFlow in GCP provides the tools you need to create and deploy machine learning models efficiently.

7.4 Leveraging AutoML for Automated Model Training

AUTOML, OR AUTOMATED Machine Learning, is a powerful tool within Google Cloud Platform (GCP) that simplifies the process of training machine learning models. It's designed for users with varying levels of expertise in machine learning, from beginners to experts. AutoML automates many of the complex and time-consuming tasks involved in model development, making it easier and more accessible.

Key Features of AutoML

AUTOML OFFERS SEVERAL key features that set it apart:

1. **Automated Model Selection**: AutoML automatically selects the most suitable model architecture for your dataset and problem, saving you the effort of manually choosing the right algorithm.
2. **Hyperparameter Tuning**: It optimizes model hyperparameters, such as learning rates and batch sizes, to achieve the best performance.
3. **Data Preprocessing**: AutoML handles data preprocessing

tasks like feature scaling and encoding, allowing you to focus on higher-level aspects of your model.

4. **AutoML Vision, Natural Language, and Tables**: Google offers specialized AutoML products for computer vision, natural language processing, and tabular data, making it easy to work with different types of data.

Using AutoML in GCP

HERE'S HOW YOU CAN leverage AutoML in GCP:

1. **Data Preparation**: Begin by preparing your dataset. Ensure it's well-structured and labeled, as AutoML relies on high-quality labeled data for training.
2. **Select AutoML Product**: Choose the appropriate AutoML product based on your data type and problem. For instance, if you're working with images, you can use AutoML Vision; for text, you can use AutoML Natural Language.
3. **Upload Data**: Upload your prepared dataset to GCP, typically in Google Cloud Storage. AutoML services can access data stored there.
4. **Define Your Problem**: Configure your AutoML model by specifying the type of problem you want to solve (e.g., image classification, sentiment analysis) and other parameters.
5. **Initiate Training**: Start the training process. AutoML will automatically explore different model architectures and hyperparameters to find the best-performing model.
6. **Evaluate Model**: Once training is complete, evaluate the model's performance using validation data. AutoML provides metrics to assess accuracy, precision, recall, etc.
7. **Deployment**: After you're satisfied with the model's

performance, you can deploy it for inference. AutoML makes it easy to create endpoints for making predictions.

8. **Monitoring and Maintenance**: Continuously monitor the model's performance and retrain it as needed to ensure it remains accurate over time.

Benefits of AutoML

AUTOML OFFERS SEVERAL advantages:

- **Accessibility**: It democratizes machine learning by allowing users without deep ML expertise to build and deploy models.

- **Efficiency**: AutoML automates many labor-intensive tasks, reducing development time and effort.

- **Accuracy**: By exploring various model architectures and hyperparameters, AutoML often produces highly accurate models.

- **Scalability**: It can handle large datasets and scale to meet the demands of production environments.

- **Flexibility**: AutoML can be used for various applications, from image recognition to text analysis.

AutoML is a valuable tool for businesses and developers looking to harness the power of machine learning without the complexities of manual model development. It streamlines the process and empowers users to create accurate and effective models for a wide range of tasks.

7.5 Case Studies: Real-World Applications of

GCP AI

IN THIS SECTION, WE will explore real-world case studies that showcase the practical applications of Google Cloud Platform (GCP) AI services. These case studies demonstrate how organizations leverage GCP's AI capabilities to solve complex problems, improve efficiency, and drive innovation in various industries.

1. Healthcare and Medical Imaging

CHALLENGE: A leading healthcare institution faced the challenge of analyzing vast volumes of medical images like X-rays, MRIs, and CT scans for diagnosis. The manual interpretation of these images was time-consuming and error-prone.

Solution: The institution adopted GCP's AI services, including AutoML Vision and TensorFlow, to build custom image recognition models. These models could quickly and accurately identify anomalies and diseases in medical images.

Outcome: By automating image analysis, the healthcare facility significantly reduced diagnosis time, improved accuracy, and enhanced patient care. Doctors could make faster decisions, leading to better patient outcomes.

2. Customer Support and Chatbots

CHALLENGE: A global e-commerce company faced a high volume of customer inquiries through various channels, making it challenging to provide timely support. They needed a solution to automate responses and assist customers efficiently.

Solution: The company implemented GCP's Dialogflow, a natural language processing (NLP) tool, to create intelligent chatbots. These chatbots could understand customer queries and provide relevant responses in real-time.

Outcome: With AI-powered chatbots, the e-commerce company reduced response times, improved customer satisfaction, and streamlined its customer support operations. Customers received quicker assistance, leading to increased sales and loyalty.

3. Fraud Detection in Banking

CHALLENGE: A major bank was grappling with a rising number of fraudulent transactions in its credit card system. Traditional rule-based fraud detection systems struggled to keep up with evolving fraud tactics.

Solution: The bank integrated GCP's AI services, including BigQuery and machine learning models, to analyze transaction data in real-time. The AI models could detect unusual patterns and flag potentially fraudulent transactions.

Outcome: By harnessing AI for fraud detection, the bank achieved a significant reduction in false positives and accurately identified fraudulent activities. This led to substantial cost savings and improved security for customers.

4. Content Recommendation in Media

CHALLENGE: A media streaming platform wanted to enhance user engagement by providing personalized content recommendations. They needed a solution that could analyze user preferences and suggest relevant content.

Solution: The platform adopted GCP's recommendation engine and used AI algorithms to analyze user behavior and preferences.

This allowed them to create personalized content playlists and recommendations.

Outcome: With AI-driven content recommendations, the media platform increased user engagement, retention, and content consumption. Users enjoyed a more tailored viewing experience, leading to higher customer satisfaction.

5. Manufacturing Quality Control

CHALLENGE: A manufacturing company faced quality control issues on its production line, resulting in defects and product recalls. They needed a solution to detect defects in real-time and minimize production errors.

Solution: The company implemented GCP's AI Vision and IoT capabilities to deploy cameras and sensors on the production line. AI models analyzed images and sensor data to identify defects instantly.

Outcome: By leveraging AI for quality control, the manufacturing company reduced defects, minimized product recalls, and improved overall product quality. This resulted in cost savings and enhanced brand reputation.

These case studies demonstrate the versatility and impact of GCP's AI services across various industries. Organizations can leverage AI to solve complex challenges, automate tasks, improve decision-making, and deliver better experiences to customers and users. As AI continues to advance, its applications in real-world scenarios will only expand, driving innovation and efficiency across different sectors.

Chapter 8: Networking and Security

8.1 Advanced Networking Concepts in GCP

IN THIS SECTION, WE will delve into advanced networking concepts within Google Cloud Platform (GCP). GCP offers a wide range of networking features and services that enable users to build robust and secure network architectures. Understanding these concepts is crucial for optimizing network performance, ensuring security, and managing complex cloud environments.

1. Virtual Private Cloud (VPC)

GOOGLE CLOUD'S VIRTUAL Private Cloud (VPC) is the foundation for building scalable and isolated network environments. With VPC, you can create your own logically isolated network within GCP. Key concepts related to VPC include:

- **Subnets**: Subnets allow you to divide your VPC's IP address range into smaller, manageable segments. You can place resources like virtual machines (VMs) or Kubernetes clusters in specific subnets.

- **Firewall Rules**: GCP provides a powerful firewall service that allows you to define rules for controlling traffic to and from your resources. Firewall rules are crucial for network security.

- **Routes**: Routes determine how network traffic is directed within your VPC. You can configure custom routes to optimize traffic flow.

2. Load Balancers

LOAD BALANCING IS ESSENTIAL for distributing incoming network traffic across multiple instances or resources to ensure high availability and reliability. GCP offers various load balancing options, including:

- **HTTP(S) Load Balancing**: Ideal for web applications, it distributes HTTP and HTTPS traffic to backend instances.

- **TCP/UDP Load Balancing**: Handles non-HTTP traffic, making it suitable for various applications.

- **Network Load Balancing**: Works at the network layer and can distribute traffic to instances in different regions.

3. Cloud DNS

GOOGLE CLOUD DNS PROVIDES a reliable, scalable, and globally distributed Domain Name System (DNS) service. It allows you to manage domain names and their associated DNS records efficiently. Some key features include:

- **Managed DNS Zones**: You can create and manage DNS zones for your domains, ensuring DNS resolution for your services.

- **Global Anycast IP Addresses**: Google Cloud DNS uses anycast IP addresses, ensuring low-latency DNS responses globally.

4. Interconnects and VPNs

INTERCONNECTS AND VPNS enable you to connect your on-premises network to Google Cloud. This is crucial for creating hybrid cloud environments or ensuring secure data transfer. Key components include:

- **Dedicated Interconnect**: Provides direct, dedicated connections between your on-premises data center and GCP.
- **Partner Interconnect**: Allows you to connect to GCP through supported service providers.
- **Cloud VPN**: Creates secure IPsec VPN connections between your on-premises network and GCP VPCs.

5. Cloud Armor and Web Application Firewalls (WAF)

SECURITY IS A TOP PRIORITY in GCP. Cloud Armor and WAF services help protect your applications and services from web threats and attacks. These services provide features like:

- **DDoS Protection**: Mitigating Distributed Denial of Service (DDoS) attacks to ensure service availability.
- **Application Layer Protection**: Filtering and inspecting traffic at the application layer to block malicious requests.
- **Rule-Based Security Policies**: Defining custom security policies to control access to your resources.

Understanding these advanced networking concepts is essential for designing secure, efficient, and highly available network architectures in Google Cloud Platform. Whether you're building a simple web application or a complex multi-region deployment, GCP's networking features can help you achieve your goals while maintaining the highest level of security and performance.

8.2 Ensuring Security and Compliance in the Cloud

ENSURING SECURITY AND compliance is a fundamental aspect of managing your infrastructure in the cloud. Google Cloud Platform (GCP) offers a robust set of tools and services to help you protect your resources and adhere to industry regulations and best practices.

1. Identity and Access Management (IAM)

IAM IS AT THE CORE of GCP's security model. It allows you to control who has access to your resources and what actions they can perform. Key IAM concepts include:

- **Users**: Individuals who use GCP resources and need specific permissions.
- **Service Accounts**: Non-human entities (e.g., applications and services) that require permissions.
- **Roles**: Sets of permissions that define what actions users and service accounts can perform.
- **Policies**: Rules that grant or deny access to resources based on roles and members.

2. Security Policies

SECURITY POLICIES IN GCP help you define and enforce security standards across your organization. Some security policy components include:

- **Organization Policies**: Enforce organization-wide constraints on resource configurations to meet compliance requirements.

- **VPC Service Controls**: Extend your Virtual Private Cloud (VPC) boundaries to protect sensitive data.

- **Data Loss Prevention (DLP)**: Identify and protect sensitive data from being leaked.

3. Key Management Service (KMS)

KMS ALLOWS YOU TO MANAGE cryptographic keys for your applications and services. You can use KMS to:

- Encrypt data at rest and in transit.

- Securely manage and rotate keys.

- Integrate with various GCP services for encryption.

4. Security Command Center

SECURITY COMMAND CENTER provides a unified security and risk management platform for GCP. It offers:

- **Security Health Analytics**: Scans your GCP resources for vulnerabilities and provides recommendations for remediation.

- **Event Threat Detection**: Detects and responds to threats and suspicious activities in real-time.

5. Compliance and Audit Logging

GCP PROVIDES COMPREHENSIVE audit logging and compliance capabilities. You can:

- Access audit logs for all activity in your GCP projects.
- Use Google Cloud's Compliance Reports to assess your compliance with industry standards and regulations.

6. Security Best Practices

ADHERING TO SECURITY best practices is essential. Some recommendations include:

- Regularly update and patch your VM instances.
- Use IAM principles of least privilege.
- Enable multi-factor authentication (MFA) for user accounts.
- Implement network segmentation and firewall rules.
- Continuously monitor and audit your environment.
- Encrypt sensitive data both at rest and in transit.

By implementing these security measures and leveraging GCP's security services, you can create a secure and compliant cloud environment for your applications and data. Security is an ongoing process, and staying informed about the latest threats and best practices is essential to protect your assets in the cloud.

8.3 Cloud Armor and Web Application Firewalls

IN THE WORLD OF CLOUD computing, security is paramount. Google Cloud Platform (GCP) provides several tools and services to safeguard your applications and infrastructure, and one of the critical components is Cloud Armor and Web Application Firewalls (WAFs).

1. Cloud Armor

CLOUD ARMOR is a managed Distributed Denial of Service (DDoS) protection and Web Application Firewall (WAF) service that defends your applications against a variety of internet threats. Here are some key features and concepts:

- **Security Policies**: You can create security policies that define rules for allowing or denying traffic based on IP addresses, geolocation, and other criteria.

- **Preconfigured Rules**: Cloud Armor provides preconfigured security rulesets to protect against common attacks like SQL injection and cross-site scripting (XSS).

- **DDoS Protection**: It offers built-in DDoS protection to mitigate large-scale attacks, ensuring your applications remain accessible.

2. Web Application Firewalls (WAFs)

A **Web Application Firewall (WAF)** is a security system designed to protect web applications from various types of attacks, including SQL injection, cross-site scripting (XSS), and other application-layer attacks. GCP integrates Cloud Armor with WAF capabilities, providing robust protection for your applications.

Key Features of Cloud Armor WAF:

- **Layer 7 Filtering**: It operates at the application layer (Layer 7) of the OSI model, inspecting and filtering HTTP and HTTPS requests.
- **Rule Sets**: You can create custom rules or use preconfigured rule sets to block or allow specific types of traffic.
- **Bot Management**: Cloud Armor can help you distinguish between legitimate traffic and malicious bots, allowing you to block or rate-limit bots as needed.
- **Logging and Monitoring**: You can log and monitor traffic that matches specific rules, helping you understand and respond to potential threats.

3. Use Cases

CLOUD ARMOR AND WAFS are essential for protecting your web applications and APIs. Some common use cases include:

- **Mitigating DDoS Attacks**: Cloud Armor helps you withstand large-scale DDoS attacks by intelligently filtering traffic and allowing legitimate requests to pass through.
- **Application Security**: Protecting your applications from known and unknown threats is critical. WAFs can

detect and block various types of attacks that target vulnerabilities in your web applications.

• **API Protection**: If you expose APIs to external clients, a WAF can secure these endpoints, ensuring only authorized access and preventing abuse.

4. Getting Started

TO GET STARTED WITH Cloud Armor and WAFs in GCP:

1. Create a security policy in the GCP Console and define your rules.
2. Attach the security policy to the backend services or resources you want to protect.
3. Monitor and tune your policies to adapt to changing traffic patterns and threats.

Remember that security is an ongoing process, and it's crucial to stay updated with the latest security threats and best practices to keep your applications and data safe in the cloud. Cloud Armor and WAFs are powerful tools in your security arsenal, but they should be part of a broader security strategy.

8.4 Virtual Private Networks (VPNs) and Interconnect

VIRTUAL PRIVATE NETWORKS (VPNs) and Interconnect are essential components of networking in Google Cloud Platform (GCP). They play a crucial role in connecting your on-premises infrastructure or remote data centers to GCP, providing secure and reliable communication between your resources.

1. Virtual Private Networks (VPNs)

VIRTUAL PRIVATE NETWORKS (VPNs) in GCP offer secure communication over the public internet. They establish encrypted connections between your on-premises network and GCP, allowing data to traverse securely.

Key Aspects of GCP VPNs:

- **Site-to-Site VPN**: This type of VPN connects your on-premises network to GCP via an encrypted tunnel over the internet. It's suitable for extending your on-premises data center to GCP.

- **Remote Access VPN**: Remote access VPNs are used for secure connections by remote users or devices to GCP resources. This is ideal for remote workers who need access to GCP services.

- **IPsec Encryption**: VPNs in GCP typically use IPsec (Internet Protocol Security) to encrypt and secure data traffic.

2. Dedicated Interconnect

DEDICATED INTERCONNECT is a private, high-bandwidth connection between your on-premises network and GCP. Unlike VPNs, it provides a direct physical link, which offers more predictable and reliable network performance.

Key Aspects of Dedicated Interconnect:

- **Private Connection**: It provides a private, dedicated connection to GCP, ensuring that your data doesn't traverse the public internet.

- **High Bandwidth**: You can choose different bandwidth options based on your needs, ranging from 50 Mbps to multiple Gbps.

- **Reduced Latency**: Dedicated Interconnect reduces latency compared to VPNs, making it suitable for latency-sensitive applications.

3. Cloud Interconnect

CLOUD INTERCONNECT is a broader term that encompasses Dedicated Interconnect and other options for connecting to GCP. It offers flexibility in choosing the right connectivity solution for your organization's requirements.

Types of Cloud Interconnect:

- **Dedicated Interconnect**: As mentioned earlier, this provides a private, high-bandwidth link.

- **Partner Interconnect**: Partner Interconnect allows you to connect to GCP via supported service providers, offering additional options for connectivity.

- **Direct Peering**: Direct Peering establishes a direct network connection to Google, providing access to various Google services.

- **Carrier Peering**: Carrier Peering connects to Google via a supported carrier, offering an alternative to Partner Interconnect.

4. Choosing Between VPNs and Interconnect

THE CHOICE BETWEEN VPNs and Interconnect depends on your specific use case and requirements:

- Use VPNs when you need a cost-effective and secure connection between your on-premises network and GCP, and you don't require high bandwidth or low latency.

- Choose Dedicated Interconnect or other Cloud Interconnect options when you need high bandwidth, low latency, and guaranteed network performance. This is especially important for mission-critical applications.

5. Setting Up VPNs and Interconnect

SETTING UP VPNS AND Interconnect involves several steps, including provisioning the necessary resources, configuring routing, and establishing security policies. Google Cloud offers detailed documentation and guides to help you through the setup process.

In conclusion, Virtual Private Networks (VPNs) and Interconnect are fundamental components for connecting your on-premises infrastructure to Google Cloud Platform. They provide secure and reliable communication, enabling you to extend your network and access GCP resources seamlessly. The choice between VPNs and Interconnect depends on your specific requirements, and GCP offers flexibility to cater to various use cases.

8.5 Best Practices for Network and Security

Management

EFFECTIVE NETWORK AND security management in Google Cloud Platform (GCP) is crucial for maintaining a secure and well-performing cloud environment. This section explores best practices and recommendations for managing your GCP network and security effectively.

1. Implement Network Segmentation

- **VPC Design**: Use Virtual Private Clouds (VPCs) to segment your network into isolated environments. Each VPC can have its own set of subnets, allowing you to control traffic flow between different components.

- **Firewall Rules**: Implement granular firewall rules to control traffic between subnets and restrict access based on specific criteria, such as IP addresses and ports.

2. Follow the Principle of Least Privilege

- **IAM Policies**: Apply the principle of least privilege to Identity and Access Management (IAM) policies. Only grant users and services the permissions they need to perform their tasks, reducing the risk of unauthorized access.

3. Use Identity and Access Management (IAM) Roles

- **IAM Roles**: Assign predefined IAM roles to users and services. Google provides a range of roles with specific permissions, making it easier to manage access control.

- **Custom Roles**: Create custom IAM roles when predefined roles don't meet your requirements. This allows for fine-grained control over permissions.

4. Enable Multi-Factor Authentication (MFA)

- **MFA**: Require Multi-Factor Authentication (MFA) for user accounts to add an extra layer of security. Users must provide two or more authentication factors before gaining access.

5. Regularly Monitor and Audit Resources

- **Logging and Monitoring**: Enable logging and monitoring for your GCP resources. Use Google Cloud's tools like Cloud Monitoring, Cloud Logging, and Cloud Audit Logs to gain visibility into resource activities and security events.

6. Use Google Cloud Security Features

- **Security Command Center**: Leverage Google Cloud Security Command Center to gain insights into the security posture of your GCP environment. It provides vulnerability assessment, threat detection, and security recommendations.

- **Cloud Armor**: Implement Web Application Firewall (WAF) policies using Cloud Armor to protect your applications from web threats and DDoS attacks.

7. Encrypt Data in Transit and at Rest

• **TLS/SSL**: Use Transport Layer Security (TLS) and Secure Sockets Layer (SSL) to encrypt data in transit. Ensure that all communication with your GCP resources is encrypted.

• **Cloud Key Management Service (KMS)**: Use Cloud KMS to manage encryption keys and encrypt data at rest, including data stored in Cloud Storage, Bigtable, and other services.

8. Regularly Review and Update Security Policies

• **Security Assessment**: Conduct regular security assessments and reviews of your GCP environment to identify vulnerabilities and compliance gaps.

• **Policy Updates**: Update security policies and configurations as needed to address new threats and adhere to best practices.

9. Disaster Recovery and Incident Response

• **Disaster Recovery Plan**: Develop a comprehensive disaster recovery plan that includes data backup, replication, and failover strategies.

• **Incident Response Plan**: Prepare an incident response plan to handle security incidents effectively. Define roles, responsibilities, and procedures for incident detection, containment, and resolution.

10. Employee Training and Awareness

- **Security Training**: Provide security training and awareness programs for your employees and users to educate them about security best practices and potential threats.

IMPLEMENTING THESE best practices will help you establish a strong network and security management framework in GCP. Keep in mind that security is an ongoing process, and staying informed about the latest security trends and updates in GCP is essential to maintaining a secure cloud environment. Regularly review and adapt your security measures to address new threats and challenges as they arise.

Chapter 9: Cloud Storage and Data Transfer

9.1 In-depth Look at Cloud Storage Options

IN GOOGLE CLOUD PLATFORM (GCP), cloud storage plays a pivotal role in storing and managing data. This section provides an in-depth exploration of the various cloud storage options available within GCP.

1. Google Cloud Storage

GOOGLE CLOUD STORAGE is a highly scalable and durable object storage service. It is suitable for a wide range of use cases, from serving website content to storing large datasets for analytics. Key features of Google Cloud Storage include:

- **Buckets**: Data is organized into buckets, which are containers for storing objects. Each bucket has a globally unique name.

- **Object Versioning**: Google Cloud Storage supports object versioning, allowing you to keep multiple versions of an object and recover previous versions when needed.

- **Access Control**: Fine-grained access control is possible through Identity and Access Management (IAM) roles and bucket-level permissions.

- **Data Lifecycle Management**: Define rules for automatically transitioning or deleting objects based on their age or other criteria.

2. Cloud Storage Classes

GOOGLE CLOUD STORAGE offers different storage classes, each designed for specific use cases and cost-efficiency:

- **Standard Storage**: Suitable for frequently accessed data with low-latency requirements.
- **Nearline Storage**: Designed for data that is accessed less frequently but requires rapid access when needed.
- **Coldline Storage**: Ideal for archival data with rare access requirements.
- **Archive Storage**: The most cost-effective option for long-term archival of data that may never be accessed.

3. Cloud Filestore

CLOUD FILESTORE IS a managed file storage service for applications that require a file system interface. It offers high performance and low latency for workloads that rely on file sharing.

- **NFS and SMB Support**: Cloud Filestore supports both NFS (Network File System) and SMB (Server Message Block) protocols.
- **Data Consistency**: Provides strong data consistency, making it suitable for applications with critical data requirements.
- **Snapshots**: You can create snapshots of your file system to capture its state at a specific point in time.

4. Persistent Disks

PERSISTENT DISKS PROVIDE block storage for virtual machine instances running on Google Compute Engine. Key features include:

- **High Performance**: Persistent Disks offer high I/O performance, making them suitable for databases and other I/O-intensive workloads.

- **Snapshots and Backups**: You can create snapshots of Persistent Disks to back up your data and restore it when needed.

- **Auto-Resize**: Persistent Disks can be resized without detaching them from virtual machines.

5. Cloud Transfer Service

THE CLOUD TRANSFER Service simplifies the process of moving data from on-premises data centers or other cloud providers to Google Cloud Storage. It supports one-time transfers and scheduled recurring transfers.

- **Transfer Options**: You can use the service for online transfers, offline transfers using physical storage devices, or transfers from other cloud providers.

- **Preservation of Metadata**: Metadata associated with your data is preserved during transfers.

- **Scheduling**: Plan and automate data transfers to minimize downtime and optimize data migration.

Understanding these cloud storage options within GCP allows you to make informed decisions about the storage solutions that best suit your specific use cases. Whether you need high-performance storage for virtual machines or cost-effective archival storage for long-term data retention, GCP provides a range of options to meet your storage needs.

9.2 Data Transfer Services and Solutions

IN GOOGLE CLOUD PLATFORM (GCP), efficiently transferring data to and from the cloud is a critical aspect of many applications and workflows. GCP offers various data transfer services and solutions to meet different data migration and transfer needs. This section provides an overview of these services and solutions.

1. Cloud Storage Transfer Service

THE CLOUD STORAGE TRANSFER Service is designed for transferring data from other cloud providers or on-premises data centers to Google Cloud Storage. Key features of this service include:

- **Scheduling**: You can schedule recurring transfers to keep your data synchronized.

- **Preservation of Metadata**: Metadata associated with your data, such as timestamps and permissions, is preserved during transfers.

- **Filtering and Exclusion**: You can specify rules to filter and exclude certain files or directories during the transfer.

- **Logging and Monitoring**: The service provides logs and monitoring capabilities to track the progress of transfers.

2. Transfer Appliance

FOR LARGE-SCALE DATA transfers where the internet may not be practical, GCP offers the Transfer Appliance. This physical device allows you to transfer large volumes of data by shipping the appliance to Google for data ingestion.

- **High Capacity**: Transfer Appliances are available in different capacities to suit your data transfer needs, from tens of terabytes to multiple petabytes.

- **Security**: Data transferred using Transfer Appliances is encrypted to ensure security during transport.

- **Offline Data Transfer**: This option is ideal for situations where transferring data over the internet is time-consuming or cost-prohibitive.

3. Cloud Data Transfer Services

GOOGLE CLOUD OFFERS specialized data transfer services for various use cases:

- **BigQuery Data Transfer Service**: This service automates the transfer of data from popular SaaS applications and data sources into Google BigQuery for analysis.

- **Cloud Dataprep**: Cloud Dataprep is a data preparation service that helps you clean, structure, and prepare your data for analysis.

- **Transfer for Online**: This service helps you transfer data from Google Drive and Google Workspace accounts to Google Cloud Storage for centralized management and analysis.

4. Cloud CDN for Content Delivery

GOOGLE CLOUD CDN (CONTENT Delivery Network) accelerates content delivery to users globally by caching content at Google's edge locations. This reduces latency and improves the user experience for web applications and media distribution.

- **Edge Caching**: Content is cached at strategically located edge nodes, reducing the load on origin servers.

- **HTTPS Load Balancing**: Google Cloud CDN integrates seamlessly with HTTPS load balancing for secure and efficient content delivery.

- **DDoS Protection**: The CDN provides protection against Distributed Denial of Service (DDoS) attacks.

5. Data Transfer Pricing

IT'S ESSENTIAL TO CONSIDER data transfer pricing when planning data transfers within GCP. Data transfer costs vary based on factors such as the source/destination, regions, and the amount of data transferred. You can use the Google Cloud Pricing Calculator to estimate data transfer costs for your specific use case.

In conclusion, Google Cloud Platform offers a range of data transfer services and solutions to facilitate efficient data migration and management. Whether you need to transfer data from on-premises environments, other cloud providers, or automate data transfers from SaaS applications, GCP provides the tools and services to meet your data transfer requirements. Understanding these options allows you to design data transfer strategies that align with your organization's needs and budget.

9.3 Cold Storage: Understanding and Using Cloud Storage Nearline and Coldline

IN GOOGLE CLOUD PLATFORM (GCP), data storage solutions cater to various use cases and performance requirements. While hot storage solutions like Standard and Nearline storage are suitable for frequently accessed data, cold storage options such as Nearline and Coldline storage are designed for cost-effective, long-term archival of data. This section focuses on understanding and using these cold storage options in GCP.

1. Cloud Storage Nearline

CLOUD STORAGE NEARLINE is a storage class in Google Cloud Storage that is optimized for data that is accessed less frequently but needs to be readily available when needed. Key characteristics of Nearline storage include:

- **Access Time**: Nearline storage offers a 30-day minimum storage duration, making it suitable for data that you anticipate needing at least once a month.

- **Cost-Effective**: While it offers faster access times compared to Coldline storage, Nearline storage is cost-effective, making it suitable for backup and archival use cases.

- **Data Retrieval**: Retrieving data from Nearline storage is slightly more expensive and may take a few seconds, making it suitable for non-critical, occasional access.

- **Data Durability**: Nearline storage provides the same high level of data durability as Standard storage classes.

2. Cloud Storage Coldline

CLOUD STORAGE COLDLINE is another storage class in Google Cloud Storage designed for long-term archival of data that is accessed very infrequently. Key features of Coldline storage include:

- **Access Time**: Coldline storage has a 90-day minimum storage duration, making it suitable for data that you expect to access less than once a quarter.

- **Lowest Cost**: Coldline storage offers the lowest storage cost among all storage classes in Google Cloud Storage. It is designed for maximum cost savings for archival data.

- **Data Retrieval**: Retrieving data from Coldline storage is more expensive and can take several hours, making it suitable for data that is rarely accessed.

- **Data Durability**: Coldline storage provides the same high level of data durability as other storage classes.

3. Use Cases for Nearline and Coldline Storage

UNDERSTANDING THE USE cases for Nearline and Coldline storage is essential to make the most of these cost-effective storage options:

- **Backup and Archival**: Nearline and Coldline storage are ideal for storing backups, archives, and historical data that may be required for compliance or auditing purposes.

- **Media Content**: For media companies and entertainment industries, long-term storage of video and audio content is cost-effective with Coldline storage.

- **Regulatory Compliance**: Businesses in regulated industries can use Coldline storage to store data for extended periods to meet compliance requirements.

- **Data Retention**: When you have data that must be retained for legal or business reasons but is unlikely to be accessed frequently, Coldline storage is a cost-effective choice.

4. Cost Considerations

WHEN USING NEARLINE and Coldline storage, it's crucial to factor in the cost considerations associated with retrieval and storage. While storage costs are lower, data retrieval from Coldline storage can incur higher costs compared to Nearline storage. It's essential to balance cost savings with retrieval time requirements based on your specific use case.

In conclusion, Google Cloud Storage offers Nearline and Coldline storage classes that are optimized for cost-effective, long-term data archival. Understanding the characteristics, access times, and use cases for these storage classes allows organizations to make informed decisions about how to store and manage their data efficiently in GCP. By selecting the right storage class for each type of data, you can optimize costs while ensuring data availability and durability.

9.4 Implementing Effective Data Backup Strategies

DATA IS ONE OF THE most valuable assets for any organization, and ensuring its safety and availability is paramount. Implementing effective data backup strategies is crucial to protect against data loss due to various factors such as hardware failures, human errors, cyberattacks, and natural disasters. In Google Cloud Platform (GCP), you can leverage a range of tools and services to create robust data backup solutions tailored to your organization's needs.

1. Use Cloud Storage for Data Backup

GOOGLE CLOUD STORAGE is a versatile and reliable object storage service that can be a cornerstone of your data backup strategy. Here are some key benefits of using Cloud Storage for data backups:

- **Durability**: Google Cloud Storage offers high data durability, ensuring that your backups are safe and available when needed.

- **Scalability**: You can scale your storage capacity as your data backup requirements grow, eliminating the need for hardware upgrades.

- **Security**: Cloud Storage provides robust security features, including encryption at rest and in transit, to protect your backup data.

- **Versioning**: Take advantage of versioning to keep historical versions of your backup data, making it easier to recover from accidental data loss.

2. Use Cloud Storage Classes

IN GCP, YOU CAN OPTIMIZE the cost of data backup by using the appropriate storage class. Consider the following:

- **Standard Storage**: Use Standard storage for frequently accessed backups or data that requires low-latency access.

- **Nearline Storage**: For data backups that are accessed less frequently but need to be readily available, Nearline storage offers a cost-effective option.

- **Coldline Storage**: Choose Coldline storage for long-term archival of backups or data that you rarely expect to access. It offers the lowest cost among storage classes.

3. Backup Automation

AUTOMATING YOUR DATA backup processes is essential to ensure consistency and reduce the risk of human error. Google Cloud offers several tools for automating backups:

- **Cloud Scheduler**: Schedule regular backup jobs to run at specific intervals using Cloud Scheduler. You can define when and how often backups should occur.

- **Cloud Functions**: Create Cloud Functions that trigger backup processes in response to specific events or changes in your data. For example, you can automatically back up data when it's modified.

- **Cloud Composer**: Use Cloud Composer to orchestrate complex backup workflows, including data extraction, transformation, and storage.

4. Data Encryption

ENSURE THAT YOUR BACKUP data is encrypted to protect it from unauthorized access. Google Cloud offers encryption options for data at rest and in transit:

- **Customer-Managed Encryption Keys (CMEK)**: Use CMEK to manage and control the encryption keys for your backup data stored in Google Cloud Storage. This provides an additional layer of security.

- **TLS/SSL**: Encrypt data in transit using Transport Layer Security (TLS) or Secure Sockets Layer (SSL) protocols when transferring backup data to and from Google Cloud Storage.

5. Regular Testing and Restoration

A BACKUP STRATEGY IS only effective if you can successfully restore data when needed. Regularly test your backup and restoration processes to ensure they work as expected. Consider the following best practices:

- Conduct periodic recovery drills to verify that you can restore data in a timely manner.

• Document and maintain clear procedures for data restoration, including any dependencies and configurations.

• Keep a record of successful backups and test restores to track the integrity of your backup data.

• Monitor backup jobs and set up alerts to detect any issues or failures in the backup process.

In conclusion, implementing effective data backup strategies in Google Cloud Platform is essential to safeguard your organization's data assets. By leveraging Google Cloud Storage, choosing the right storage classes, automating backup processes, implementing data encryption, and regularly testing data restoration, you can ensure the availability and integrity of your backup data, reducing the risk of data loss and minimizing downtime in the event of unexpected incidents.

9.5 Optimizing Costs and Performance in Data Storage

EFFICIENTLY MANAGING data storage in Google Cloud Platform (GCP) is crucial for both cost savings and maintaining optimal performance. As your organization's data volume grows, implementing strategies to optimize storage costs while ensuring data availability and performance becomes increasingly important. In this section, we will explore various techniques and best practices for achieving the balance between cost optimization and data storage performance in GCP.

1. Data Lifecycle Management

IMPLEMENTING A DATA lifecycle management strategy helps you automatically manage the lifecycle of your data based on predefined policies. Here are some key aspects to consider:

- **Data Retention Policies**: Define policies that specify how long data should be retained in active storage before transitioning to lower-cost storage classes or being deleted.

- **Automatic Deletion**: Set up automatic deletion rules for data that is no longer needed, reducing storage costs.

- **Storage Tiers**: Leverage different storage classes in Google Cloud Storage, such as Standard, Nearline, and Coldline, to move data to more cost-effective tiers as it becomes less frequently accessed.

2. Object Versioning

GOOGLE CLOUD STORAGE supports object versioning, allowing you to keep historical versions of objects. While this feature provides data protection against accidental deletions or modifications, it can also impact storage costs. Consider the following:

- **Enable Versioning Selectively**: Enable versioning only for critical objects or those that require historical tracking, rather than enabling it for all objects.

- **Manage Old Versions**: Periodically review and delete old versions of objects that are no longer needed to reduce storage costs.

3. Use of Compression and Archiving

COMPRESSING DATA BEFORE storage and archiving infrequently accessed data can significantly reduce storage costs. Here are some recommendations:

- **Data Compression**: Use compression techniques to reduce the size of data stored in Google Cloud Storage, especially for text-based or log data.

- **Archival Storage**: For data that is rarely accessed but must be retained for compliance or legal reasons, consider archiving options like Cloud Storage Nearline or Cloud Storage Coldline.

4. Data Deduplication

DEDUPLICATION IS THE process of identifying and eliminating duplicate copies of data. Implementing data deduplication can lead to significant storage savings, especially when dealing with redundant backups or datasets. Google Cloud does not natively provide data deduplication, but you can use third-party tools and scripts to deduplicate data before uploading it to Cloud Storage.

5. Monitoring and Cost Optimization Tools

GCP OFFERS SEVERAL tools and services to monitor and optimize storage costs:

- **Google Cloud Storage Cost Calculator**: Use the cost calculator to estimate your monthly storage costs based on your usage patterns and storage classes.

- **Cloud Storage Usage Reports**: Monitor and analyze your storage usage reports to identify trends and opportunities for optimization.
- **Cloud Storage Object Lifecycle Management**: Implement lifecycle policies to automate the transition of objects to different storage classes or delete them based on specific conditions.
- **Cloud Storage Cost Optimization Recommendations**: Leverage the built-in recommendations to optimize your storage costs.

6. Consider Object Metadata

WHEN STORING OBJECTS in Google Cloud Storage, consider using object metadata to add custom information to your objects. This can help with data organization and retrieval. However, be mindful of metadata size, as it can impact storage costs.

7. Use Case-Specific Strategies

THE BEST APPROACH TO optimizing costs and performance in data storage may vary depending on your specific use case and data access patterns. It's essential to analyze your data storage requirements and design a strategy that aligns with your organization's goals.

In conclusion, optimizing costs and performance in data storage within Google Cloud Platform is an ongoing process that requires careful planning and management. By implementing data lifecycle policies, utilizing storage classes effectively, enabling object versioning selectively, using compression and archiving where applicable, considering data deduplication, and leveraging monitoring and cost optimization tools, you can strike the right balance between cost efficiency and data availability and performance.

Chapter 10: Exploring APIs and Services

10.1 Overview of GCP's API Ecosystem

GOOGLE CLOUD PLATFORM (GCP) provides a vast ecosystem of APIs (Application Programming Interfaces) and services that enable developers to build, deploy, and scale applications with ease. In this section, we'll explore the key aspects of GCP's API ecosystem, including the types of APIs available, their importance, and how to leverage them effectively in your projects.

1. Types of APIs in GCP

GCP OFFERS A WIDE RANGE of APIs, each designed to address specific use cases and services. Here are some of the main categories of APIs available:

- **Compute APIs**: These APIs allow you to manage virtual machines, containers, and other compute resources. For example, the Compute Engine API enables you to create and manage virtual machines programmatically.

- **Storage APIs**: GCP offers APIs for various storage services, including Cloud Storage for object storage and Cloud SQL for managing relational databases.

- **AI and Machine Learning APIs**: GCP provides a suite of AI and machine learning APIs, such as the Vision AI API for image analysis and the Natural Language API for text analysis.

- **Data APIs**: These APIs enable you to interact with data-related services like BigQuery for data analytics and Firestore for NoSQL database operations.

- **Networking APIs**: GCP's networking APIs include services like Cloud DNS for managing DNS records and Load Balancing API for configuring load balancers.

- **Security and Identity APIs**: APIs like Identity and Access Management (IAM) help you manage access control and permissions in your projects.

2. Importance of GCP APIs

GCP APIS PLAY A CRUCIAL role in enabling developers to harness the power of Google's cloud infrastructure. Here's why GCP APIs are essential:

- **Automation and Orchestration**: APIs allow you to automate tasks and orchestrate complex workflows, making it easier to manage cloud resources programmatically.

- **Integration**: GCP APIs facilitate seamless integration with other services and platforms, enabling you to build hybrid and multi-cloud solutions.

- **Scalability**: APIs enable your applications to scale dynamically based on demand, ensuring optimal performance and resource utilization.

- **Customization**: With APIs, you can customize and extend the functionality of GCP services to suit your specific requirements.

3. Authentication and Authorization

TO INTERACT WITH GCP APIs securely, you need to implement proper authentication and authorization mechanisms. GCP offers various authentication methods, including service account keys, OAuth 2.0, and Identity Platform, to ensure that only authorized entities access your resources.

4. API Documentation and Libraries

GOOGLE PROVIDES COMPREHENSIVE documentation for each API, including reference guides, tutorials, and sample code. Additionally, GCP offers client libraries for various programming languages, simplifying API integration and development.

5. API Management

GCP PROVIDES TOOLS like Cloud Endpoints and Apigee for API management, allowing you to publish, secure, and monitor your APIs effectively.

In summary, GCP's API ecosystem empowers developers to build scalable, integrated, and customized cloud solutions. Whether you need to manage infrastructure, analyze data, incorporate AI and machine learning capabilities, or enhance security, GCP's APIs provide the tools and flexibility to achieve your goals. In the following sections, we'll delve deeper into specific API integrations and strategies for leveraging GCP's API ecosystem effectively in your projects.

10.2 Integrating Google Maps and Other Google APIs

GOOGLE CLOUD PLATFORM (GCP) offers a variety of APIs, and one of the most commonly used ones is the Google Maps API. In this section, we'll explore how to integrate Google Maps and other Google APIs into your applications, whether you're building a location-based service, a mapping application, or simply enhancing the functionality of your project.

1. Google Maps API

THE GOOGLE MAPS API allows developers to embed interactive maps into their web or mobile applications. This API provides various features, such as displaying maps, adding markers, calculating directions, and geocoding. Here's a basic example of how to embed a Google Map in a web page:

```
<!DOCTYPE html>

<html>

<head>

<title>Simple Google Map</title>

<script

src="https://maps.googleapis.com/maps/api/
js?key=YOUR_API_KEY&callback=initMap"

async

defer

></script>
```

```
<script>
function initMap() {
const map = new google.maps.Map(document.getElementById("map"), {
center: { lat: -34.397, lng: 150.644 },
zoom: 8,
});
}
</script>
</head>
<body>
<div id="map" style="height: 400px; width: 100%;"></div>
</body>
</html>
```

Replace YOUR_API_KEY with your actual Google Maps API key obtained from the Google Cloud Console.

2. Google Places API

THE GOOGLE PLACES API allows you to search for places, retrieve details about places, and even add places to your application. You can use this API to implement location-based features like searching for nearby restaurants or displaying detailed information about a specific place.

3. Geocoding API

THE GEOCODING API ENABLES you to convert addresses into geographic coordinates (latitude and longitude) and vice versa. This is particularly useful when you need to work with location data in your application.

4. Directions API

THE DIRECTIONS API allows you to calculate directions and estimated travel times between locations. You can use it to build applications that provide route planning and navigation functionality.

5. Distance Matrix API

THE DISTANCE MATRIX API provides travel distance and time estimates for a matrix of origins and destinations. It's useful for applications involving logistics, delivery, or any scenario where you need to calculate distances and durations between multiple points.

6. Using Google APIs with GCP

TO USE GOOGLE MAPS and other Google APIs effectively, you'll need to create a project in the Google Cloud Console and enable the APIs you want to use. Then, you'll obtain API keys and configure them in your applications. It's essential to follow best practices for API key security and usage limits to ensure your applications run smoothly and securely.

7. Billing and Quotas

KEEP IN MIND THAT SOME Google APIs may have usage limits and associated costs. Be sure to review the pricing and quotas for the APIs you plan to use and monitor your usage to avoid unexpected charges.

In conclusion, integrating Google Maps and other Google APIs into your applications can enhance their functionality and provide valuable location-based services to your users. Whether you're building a mapping application, a ride-sharing service, or a location-aware mobile app, GCP's APIs offer the tools you need to make your project a success.

10.3 Leveraging Cloud Endpoints for API Management

APIS (APPLICATION PROGRAMMING Interfaces) are fundamental building blocks of modern software applications. They enable different software components to communicate with each other, and they play a crucial role in enabling the integration of various services and systems. Managing APIs effectively is essential for ensuring security, scalability, and ease of use. Google Cloud Platform (GCP) provides a service called **Cloud Endpoints** to help you manage and deploy APIs seamlessly.

1. What are Cloud Endpoints?

CLOUD ENDPOINTS is a fully managed service that allows you to create, deploy, and manage APIs on GCP. It offers a range of features to simplify the development and management of APIs, making it easier for developers to build and secure APIs for their applications.

2. Key Features of Cloud Endpoints

HERE ARE SOME OF THE key features and benefits of using Cloud Endpoints:

a. API Management:

CLOUD ENDPOINTS PROVIDES tools for defining and deploying APIs, including versioning and the ability to control access through API keys and authentication methods.

b. Security:

YOU CAN USE CLOUD ENDPOINTS to implement authentication and authorization mechanisms for your APIs. It supports OAuth 2.0, API keys, and Firebase Authentication for securing access.

c. Scalability:

CLOUD ENDPOINTS IS designed to handle the scaling needs of your APIs. It can automatically scale to handle increased traffic as your application grows.

d. Monitoring and Logging:

YOU CAN MONITOR THE usage of your APIs and gather insights into performance and usage patterns. Cloud Endpoints integrates with other GCP services like Stackdriver for comprehensive monitoring and logging.

e. Extensible:

CLOUD ENDPOINTS ALLOWS you to create APIs using the OpenAPI Specification (formerly known as Swagger). This makes it easy to describe your API's structure and operations.

f. Language Support:

CLOUD ENDPOINTS SUPPORTS multiple programming languages, including Python, Java, and Node.js, making it versatile and suitable for a wide range of development stacks.

3. Getting Started with Cloud Endpoints

TO GET STARTED WITH Cloud Endpoints, you typically follow these steps:

1. **Design Your API**: Define your API using the OpenAPI Specification. This includes specifying endpoints, methods, request/response schemas, and security requirements.
2. **Deploy Your API**: Use the Cloud Endpoints service to deploy your API to GCP. This step involves configuring routing, security, and other settings.
3. **Securing Your API**: Implement security measures like authentication and authorization to control access to your API.
4. **Monitoring and Optimization**: Continuously monitor the performance and usage of your API, and make optimizations as needed.
5. **Scaling**: As your API usage grows, ensure that it can scale to meet the demand. Cloud Endpoints can help with this by automatically managing the scaling process.

4. Use Cases for Cloud Endpoints

CLOUD ENDPOINTS CAN be used in a variety of scenarios, including:

- Building RESTful APIs for web and mobile applications.

- Creating APIs for microservices-based architectures.
- Exposing backend services securely to external developers or partners.
- Managing and securing APIs in a multi-cloud or hybrid cloud environment.

5. Conclusion

API MANAGEMENT IS A critical aspect of modern application development. Cloud Endpoints simplifies the process of creating, deploying, and managing APIs on Google Cloud Platform, allowing developers to focus on building their applications while ensuring scalability and security for their APIs. Whether you're building a simple RESTful API or managing a complex ecosystem of microservices, Cloud Endpoints can help streamline the process.

10.4 Understanding Apigee API Management

APIGEE IS A COMPREHENSIVE API management platform that provides tools and services for designing, securing, deploying, and monitoring APIs. It offers a range of features and capabilities to help organizations manage their API ecosystems effectively. In this section, we will explore Apigee and its key functionalities.

1. What is Apigee?

APIGEE, NOW PART OF Google Cloud, is a full-featured API management platform that enables organizations to create, manage, and analyze APIs. It acts as a gateway that sits between your backend services and the applications that consume them. Apigee provides a unified platform for API design, security, analytics, and developer collaboration.

2. Key Features of Apigee

HERE ARE SOME OF THE key features and capabilities of Apigee:

a. API Design:

APIGEE ALLOWS YOU TO design APIs using a visual, code-free interface or by importing existing API specifications (such as OpenAPI or RAML). You can define API endpoints, request/response schemas, and transformations.

b. Security:

APIGEE PROVIDES ROBUST security features, including OAuth 2.0 authentication, API key management, rate limiting, and threat protection. You can secure your APIs against unauthorized access and protect them from various security threats.

c. Analytics:

ONE OF THE STANDOUT features of Apigee is its analytics capabilities. It tracks API usage, monitors performance, and provides insights into how your APIs are being used. This data is invaluable for optimizing API performance and understanding user behavior.

d. Developer Portal:

APIGEE INCLUDES A DEVELOPER portal that allows you to create a customized, self-service portal for developers. Developers can discover your APIs, access documentation, and obtain API keys.

e. API Deployment:

YOU CAN DEPLOY APIS to Apigee's cloud-based runtime, which provides high availability and scalability. Apigee handles API traffic management, load balancing, and caching.

f. Traffic Management:

APIGEE OFFERS TRAFFIC management features like rate limiting, caching, and content negotiation to ensure optimal API performance and reliability.

g. Developer Collaboration:

APIGEE SUPPORTS DEVELOPER collaboration by providing tools for API testing, debugging, and version control. Developers can work together seamlessly on API projects.

3. Use Cases for Apigee

APIGEE CAN BE USED in various scenarios, including:

- **API Monetization**: Organizations can use Apigee to monetize their APIs by offering them as products to external developers or partners.

- **Partner Integration**: Apigee facilitates partner integration by providing a secure and controlled way for external entities to access specific APIs.

- **Microservices**: In a microservices architecture, Apigee can act as an API gateway to manage traffic, security, and versioning across microservices.

- **Legacy Systems**: Apigee can expose and modernize legacy systems by wrapping them with APIs, making them accessible to modern applications.

- **IoT**: For IoT solutions, Apigee can handle the communication between IoT devices and backend services, ensuring security and scalability.

4. Getting Started with Apigee

TO GET STARTED WITH Apigee, you typically follow these steps:

1. **API Design**: Define your APIs, specifying endpoints, request/response schemas, and security requirements.
2. **API Deployment**: Deploy your APIs to Apigee's runtime, configuring routing, security, and other settings.
3. **Security**: Implement security measures such as authentication, authorization, and threat protection to secure your APIs.
4. **Analytics**: Monitor and analyze API usage and performance using Apigee's analytics tools.
5. **Developer Portal**: Create a developer portal for developers to discover and access your APIs.

5. Conclusion

APIGEE IS A POWERFUL API management platform that simplifies the process of designing, securing, deploying, and monitoring APIs. Whether you are building APIs for internal use, partner integration, or external developers, Apigee provides the tools and features you need to manage your API ecosystem effectively. Its robust security, analytics, and developer collaboration capabilities make it a valuable asset for organizations looking to deliver high-quality APIs.

10.5 Building and Consuming APIs in GCP

IN THIS SECTION, WE'LL explore the process of building and consuming APIs (Application Programming Interfaces) within Google Cloud Platform (GCP). APIs play a crucial role in modern software development, enabling different applications to communicate and share data and functionality seamlessly.

1. Building APIs

a. API Design:

BEFORE YOU CAN BUILD an API, you need to design it. GCP offers multiple tools for designing APIs, including Google Cloud Endpoints, which allows you to create, deploy, and manage APIs using a simple and scalable approach. You can define your API's endpoints, request/response schemas, and authentication methods.

b. Cloud Endpoints:

GOOGLE CLOUD ENDPOINTS is a powerful tool for building APIs. It supports both RESTful and gRPC-based APIs. With Cloud Endpoints, you can define your API using the OpenAPI Specification (formerly known as Swagger), making it easy to generate client libraries for various programming languages.

c. Authentication and Authorization:

API SECURITY IS PARAMOUNT. GCP provides robust authentication and authorization mechanisms to protect your APIs. You can use Google Identity Platform, Firebase Authentication, or OAuth 2.0 to secure your APIs and control access.

d. Deployment and Scaling:

ONCE YOUR API IS DESIGNED, you can deploy it to Google App Engine, Google Kubernetes Engine (GKE), or Cloud Functions, depending on your application's requirements. GCP offers automatic scaling to handle traffic spikes and ensure high availability.

2. Consuming APIs

a. API Key:

TO CONSUME AN API, you often need an API key. GCP allows you to generate API keys and restrict their usage to specific IP addresses or applications. API keys are commonly used for simple authentication.

b. Client Libraries:

GOOGLE CLOUD PROVIDES client libraries for various programming languages, simplifying the process of consuming GCP services and APIs. These libraries abstract the underlying HTTP requests and authentication processes, making integration easier.

c. Service Account Credentials:

FOR SERVER-TO-SERVER communication within GCP, you can use service account credentials. Service accounts represent your applications and can be granted permissions to access GCP resources securely.

d. OAuth 2.0:

OAUTH 2.0 IS A STANDARD protocol for secure authorization. GCP supports OAuth 2.0, allowing you to implement OAuth 2.0-based authentication and authorization in your applications. This is particularly useful for third-party integrations and user authentication.

3. API Management and Monitoring

a. API Management:

GCP OFFERS TOOLS LIKE Google Cloud Endpoints and Apigee for managing your APIs. These tools provide features such as versioning, access control, rate limiting, and analytics to ensure your APIs are reliable and secure.

b. Monitoring and Logging:

TO MAINTAIN THE HEALTH and performance of your APIs, GCP offers Cloud Monitoring and Cloud Logging. You can set up alerts, view metrics, and access detailed logs to troubleshoot issues and monitor API usage.

4. Real-World Use Cases

APIS ARE USED IN A wide range of applications. Some common use cases within GCP include:

- **Web and Mobile Applications**: APIs are essential for building web and mobile applications that require access to various GCP services.

- **Data Integration**: APIs enable data integration between different systems and databases within GCP, facilitating data synchronization and reporting.

- **IoT (Internet of Things)**: IoT devices often communicate with cloud-based services via APIs to send and receive data.

- **Machine Learning**: APIs can be used to deploy machine learning models and make predictions or perform natural language processing tasks.

- **E-commerce**: APIs are crucial for e-commerce platforms to connect with payment gateways, shipping services, and inventory management systems.

5. Conclusion

BUILDING AND CONSUMING APIs are fundamental aspects of modern software development. Google Cloud Platform provides a robust ecosystem for designing, securing, deploying, and managing APIs. Whether you are creating APIs for your own applications or exposing them for third-party integrations, GCP offers the tools and services needed to ensure your APIs are performant, secure, and scalable. Understanding the principles and best practices outlined in this section will help you harness the power of APIs within GCP effectively.

Chapter 11: Scalability and Performance Optimization

Section 11.1: Principles of Scalability in the Cloud

IN THE WORLD OF CLOUD computing, scalability is a fundamental concept that plays a pivotal role in ensuring that your applications and services can meet the demands of your users effectively. Scalability refers to the ability of a system to handle an increasing workload, typically achieved by adding more resources or components to the system. In this section, we will delve into the principles of scalability in the cloud and explore the various strategies and techniques that can be employed to build scalable systems on Google Cloud Platform (GCP).

Understanding Scalability

SCALABILITY IS OFTEN categorized into two main types: horizontal scalability and vertical scalability.

Horizontal scalability involves adding more identical instances or nodes to your system. This approach is commonly referred to as "scaling out." It is a fundamental principle of many cloud-based systems. In GCP, services like Google Compute Engine allow you to easily create multiple virtual machines (VMs) to distribute the workload and improve system performance.

Vertical scalability, on the other hand, involves increasing the capacity of individual components within the system. This approach is known as "scaling up." In GCP, this can be achieved by upgrading the CPU, memory, or other resources of a VM. While vertical scalability can be effective, it may have limitations, and there may be a point where further vertical scaling becomes impractical or costly.

Key Scalability Concepts

1. Load Balancing

LOAD BALANCING IS A crucial component of scalability. It involves distributing incoming network traffic across multiple resources to ensure optimal utilization and prevent overloading of any single component. Google Cloud offers various load balancing solutions, including HTTP(S) Load Balancing, Network Load Balancing, and Internal Load Balancing, which help distribute traffic across multiple instances or services.

2. Auto-Scaling

AUTO-SCALING IS THE ability of a system to automatically adjust its capacity based on traffic or workload. GCP provides Auto Scaling, which allows you to define policies to automatically add or remove instances based on predefined conditions. This ensures that your applications can handle varying levels of load without manual intervention.

3. Distributed Architectures

SCALABLE SYSTEMS ARE often built using distributed architectures. This involves breaking down applications into smaller, loosely coupled components that can be deployed and scaled independently. GCP offers services like Kubernetes Engine (GKE) for orchestrating containerized applications in a distributed manner.

4. Statelessness

STATELESS APPLICATIONS are easier to scale because they don't rely on maintaining session state between requests. Cloud-native design principles often encourage stateless application architectures, making it easier to distribute requests across multiple instances.

Strategies for Scalability

WHEN DESIGNING FOR scalability in GCP, consider the following strategies:

1. **Microservices Architecture**: Implementing applications as a collection of small, independent microservices allows you to scale each service independently, optimizing resource usage.
2. **Caching**: Utilize caching mechanisms like Google Cloud Memorystore or Cloud CDN to reduce the load on backend systems by serving frequently accessed data from memory.
3. **Database Scaling**: Choose appropriate database solutions like Cloud Spanner or Cloud Bigtable that can scale horizontally to handle growing datasets.
4. **Serverless**: Leverage serverless computing platforms like Cloud Functions and App Engine, which automatically handle the underlying infrastructure and scale as needed based on incoming requests.
5. **Monitoring and Alerts**: Implement proactive monitoring and alerting systems to detect performance bottlenecks and trigger scaling actions when predefined thresholds are reached.
6. **Load Testing**: Regularly perform load testing to assess

your system's performance under heavy traffic and identify potential bottlenecks.

Scalability is not a one-size-fits-all solution. The appropriate scalability strategy for your application depends on factors like your workload, architecture, and business requirements. However, by understanding the principles and employing the right tools and techniques, you can ensure that your applications on GCP are capable of scaling to meet user demands efficiently and reliably.

Section 11.2: Performance Tuning and Best Practices

PERFORMANCE TUNING is a critical aspect of ensuring that your applications running on Google Cloud Platform (GCP) deliver optimal speed, responsiveness, and resource utilization. In this section, we will explore performance tuning best practices and techniques to enhance the efficiency of your cloud-based applications.

Monitoring and Profiling

BEFORE YOU CAN OPTIMIZE performance, you need to monitor and profile your applications to identify bottlenecks and areas that require improvement. GCP offers several tools and services for monitoring and profiling, including:

- **Google Cloud Monitoring**: This service provides real-time visibility into the performance of your applications and infrastructure. You can set up custom dashboards, alerts, and metrics to track specific aspects of your applications.

- **Google Cloud Profiler**: Profiler helps you understand your application's CPU and memory usage by continuously collecting and analyzing data. It can pinpoint performance bottlenecks in your code.

- **Google Cloud Trace**: Trace helps you understand the latency and performance of your applications by providing detailed insights into request processing times. You can trace requests across multiple services to identify slow components.

Optimization Techniques

ONCE YOU HAVE IDENTIFIED performance issues, you can apply various optimization techniques:

1. Code Optimization

- **Algorithmic Efficiency**: Review your code's algorithms and data structures to ensure they are as efficient as possible. Small changes in algorithms can lead to significant performance improvements.

- **Profiling and Benchmarking**: Use profiling tools to identify slow functions or code sections. Benchmarking can help you compare the performance of different code implementations.

- **Lazy Loading**: Load resources, data, or components only when they are needed, rather than loading everything upfront. This can reduce startup time and resource consumption.

2. Resource Scaling

- **Auto-Scaling**: Configure auto-scaling policies to automatically adjust resources based on traffic. This ensures that you have enough capacity during peak periods and can save costs during low traffic.

- **Vertical Scaling**: Consider vertical scaling by using larger machine types or more powerful CPUs if your application requires it. GCP provides flexibility in resizing VMs.

- **Horizontal Scaling**: Implement horizontal scaling by adding more instances or microservices to distribute workloads. Containers and Kubernetes (GKE) are useful for managing scalable applications.

3. Caching

- **Caching Layers**: Implement caching mechanisms to store frequently accessed data in memory. Use Google Cloud Memorystore or Cloud CDN for caching to reduce the load on backend services.

- **Content Delivery Networks (CDNs)**: Utilize CDNs to serve static assets and content from edge locations closer to end-users, reducing latency and improving load times.

4. Database Optimization

- **Query Optimization**: Review and optimize database queries to reduce execution times. Indexes, query caching, and query batching can help improve database performance.

- **Scaling Databases**: Choose the appropriate database service for your needs, such as Cloud SQL, Cloud Spanner, or Cloud Bigtable, and scale them horizontally or vertically based on workload.

5. Content Compression

- **Gzip Compression**: Enable Gzip compression for HTTP responses to reduce data transfer size over the network, resulting in faster page loads for web applications.

Load Testing and Benchmarking

TO VALIDATE THE EFFECTIVENESS of your performance optimizations, conduct load testing and benchmarking. Load testing simulates high levels of traffic to evaluate how your application handles heavy loads. Benchmarking compares your application's performance against industry standards or similar applications.

GCP provides tools like **Google Cloud Load Testing** and third-party solutions to help you conduct load tests and benchmarking. By analyzing the results, you can fine-tune your performance optimizations further.

Remember that performance tuning is an iterative process. Continuously monitor your application's performance, apply optimizations, and test their impact. By following these best practices and leveraging GCP's monitoring and profiling tools, you can ensure that your applications deliver optimal performance to your users.

Section 11.3: Load Testing and Auto-Scaling

LOAD TESTING AND AUTO-scaling are essential components of optimizing the performance and scalability of your applications running on Google Cloud Platform (GCP). In this section, we will explore the importance of load testing and how auto-scaling can help your applications efficiently handle varying workloads.

Load Testing

LOAD TESTING IS THE process of simulating a high volume of traffic to your application to assess its behavior under peak conditions. The primary goals of load testing are to:

1. **Identify Performance Bottlenecks**: Load testing helps you pinpoint performance bottlenecks in your application, such as slow response times, high resource utilization, or inefficient code.
2. **Determine Scalability**: By analyzing how your application scales under load, you can assess its ability to handle increased traffic and workload demands.
3. **Validate Performance Improvements**: If you've made performance optimizations, load testing can validate whether these changes have resulted in improved application performance.
4. **Plan for Capacity**: Load testing helps you plan the required capacity for your application to ensure it meets user expectations during traffic spikes or increased usage.

GCP offers tools and services that facilitate load testing, including:

- **Google Cloud Load Testing**: A service that allows you to create and execute load tests on your applications. It can simulate various user scenarios and assess application performance.

- **Google Kubernetes Engine (GKE)**: GKE enables you to deploy containerized applications and services. You can use tools like Kubernetes Horizontal Pod Autoscaling to automatically adjust the number of instances based on load.

- **Google Cloud Monitoring**: Monitoring provides insights into your application's performance during load testing, helping you understand resource consumption and bottlenecks.

When conducting load testing, consider factors such as the number of concurrent users, the distribution of requests, and the duration of the test. Analyze metrics like response times, error rates, and resource utilization to make informed decisions about optimization.

Auto-Scaling

AUTO-SCALING IS A CRUCIAL strategy to ensure your applications can dynamically adjust resources to match varying workloads. With auto-scaling, your application infrastructure can automatically expand or contract based on predefined rules or metrics.

Key aspects of auto-scaling in GCP include:

1. **Horizontal Scaling**: This involves adding or removing instances of your application to distribute the workload. GCP provides services like Google Compute Engine Autoscaler and Kubernetes Horizontal Pod Autoscaling to automate this process.

2. **Vertical Scaling**: Vertical scaling involves changing the size of individual instances, such as increasing CPU or memory. You can adjust the machine type of virtual machines (VMs) in GCP to vertically scale resources.
3. **Load-Based Scaling**: Auto-scaling can be triggered based on metrics like CPU utilization, memory usage, or custom application metrics. When these metrics cross predefined thresholds, the system scales resources accordingly.
4. **Scheduled Scaling**: You can schedule auto-scaling events to coincide with expected traffic patterns. For example, you can increase capacity during business hours and reduce it during low-traffic periods.
5. **Container Orchestration**: If you use Kubernetes on GKE, the Kubernetes Horizontal Pod Autoscaler can automatically adjust the number of pods based on CPU or custom metrics.

Auto-scaling not only ensures that your application can handle traffic spikes but also optimizes resource usage and cost efficiency. By scaling resources dynamically, you can strike a balance between performance and cost.

When setting up auto-scaling, carefully define scaling policies, monitor the system's behavior, and refine your scaling rules as needed to achieve optimal performance and resource utilization.

In conclusion, load testing and auto-scaling are critical components of performance optimization in GCP. Load testing helps you understand your application's behavior under different workloads, while auto-scaling ensures that your infrastructure can adapt to changing demands efficiently. By leveraging these practices and GCP's tools, you can deliver a reliable and responsive user experience for your applications.

Section 11.4: Optimizing Costs in GCP

OPTIMIZING COSTS IN Google Cloud Platform (GCP) is crucial to ensuring that your cloud infrastructure remains efficient and cost-effective. In this section, we will explore various strategies and best practices for cost optimization in GCP.

1. Rightsizing Resources

ONE OF THE PRIMARY ways to optimize costs in GCP is to rightsize your resources. Rightsizing involves selecting the appropriate machine type, memory, and storage for your workloads. GCP provides tools like the Google Cloud Pricing Calculator and the Compute Engine Rightsizing Recommendations to help you make informed decisions.

2. Auto-scaling

AS DISCUSSED IN THE previous section, auto-scaling is not only beneficial for performance but also for cost optimization. Auto-scaling allows you to automatically adjust the number of instances or resources based on workload, helping you avoid over-provisioning.

3. Resource Cleanup

REGULARLY REVIEW AND clean up unused or idle resources. GCP offers tools like the Google Cloud Scheduler, which allows you to automate resource deletion based on schedules or conditions. This practice helps eliminate unnecessary costs associated with dormant resources.

4. Use Committed Use Contracts

GOOGLE CLOUD OFFERS Committed Use Contracts (CUCs), which allow you to commit to using specific VM types for a one or three-year term. This commitment provides significant cost savings compared to pay-as-you-go pricing.

5. Use Sustained Use Discounts

GCP PROVIDES SUSTAINED Use Discounts, which automatically apply discounts as you use VMs for a significant portion of the month. As your usage increases, the discount level increases, resulting in lower costs.

6. Leverage Preemptible VMs

PREEMPTIBLE VMS ARE cost-effective, short-lived instances suitable for fault-tolerant workloads. They are available at a fraction of the cost of standard VMs but come with the caveat that they can be terminated with short notice.

7. Optimize Storage

CHOOSE THE APPROPRIATE storage class for your data in Google Cloud Storage. For infrequently accessed data, consider using Nearline or Coldline storage classes to reduce storage costs.

8. Monitor and Set Alerts

USE GOOGLE CLOUD MONITORING to set up custom alerts based on specific metrics. This enables you to proactively address performance or cost issues before they become significant.

9. Budgeting and Cost Control

SET UP BUDGETS AND billing alerts in GCP's Billing section. These features help you track spending and receive alerts when your spending approaches or exceeds predefined thresholds.

10. Use Google Cloud's Cost Management Tools

GOOGLE CLOUD OFFERS various tools like Cost Explorer, Cost Allocation, and Billing Reports that provide insights into your spending patterns and enable you to allocate costs accurately.

11. Review and Optimize Licensing

REVIEW YOUR LICENSING agreements for software and services running on GCP. Some licenses may allow you to bring your own licenses (BYOL), resulting in cost savings.

12. Evaluate Service Usage

REGULARLY ASSESS YOUR usage of GCP services and consider whether there are alternative, more cost-effective solutions that meet your requirements.

13. Explore Complementary Services

GOOGLE CLOUD OFFERS a range of complementary services like Anthos, which can help optimize multi-cloud and hybrid cloud costs.

14. Cost Optimization Best Practices

KEEP UP TO DATE WITH cost optimization best practices provided by Google Cloud's Cost Optimization Guides and resources.

In conclusion, cost optimization in GCP is an ongoing process that requires proactive monitoring, evaluation, and adjustment of your cloud resources. By implementing these strategies and leveraging Google Cloud's tools, you can optimize your cloud spending while maintaining the performance and reliability of your applications.

Section 11.5: Case Studies: Scalable Architectures in GCP

IN THIS SECTION, WE will explore several real-world case studies that showcase scalable architectures implemented on Google Cloud Platform (GCP). These examples demonstrate how organizations have leveraged GCP's features to build flexible and scalable solutions to meet their specific needs.

1. Spotify: Scaling Music Streaming

SPOTIFY, A POPULAR music streaming service, relies on Google Cloud to handle massive volumes of audio data and user requests. GCP services like Google Kubernetes Engine (GKE) and Bigtable enable Spotify to scale its infrastructure dynamically, ensuring a seamless music streaming experience for millions of users worldwide.

2. Snapchat: Managing User Growth

SNAPCHAT, A MULTIMEDIA messaging app, faced rapid user growth and needed a scalable infrastructure. They turned to Google Cloud and GKE to manage containerized workloads efficiently. GKE's auto-scaling capabilities allow Snapchat to adapt to changing user demand while maintaining cost efficiency.

3. Niantic: Hosting Augmented Reality Games

NIANTIC, THE COMPANY behind Pokémon GO and other augmented reality (AR) games, uses GCP to host its gaming platforms. Google Cloud's global network and load balancing capabilities ensure low-latency gameplay for millions of users. Niantic can scale its infrastructure based on player activity during special in-game events.

4. Zynga: Supporting Online Games

ZYNGA, A MOBILE GAME developer, relies on GCP to support its online multiplayer games. Google Cloud's Compute Engine and Kubernetes Engine provide the flexibility to scale game servers up or down based on player demand. This scalability ensures a smooth gaming experience and cost savings during off-peak times.

5. Twitter: Analyzing Real-Time Data

TWITTER USES GCP TO analyze real-time data generated by its massive user base. BigQuery and Dataflow enable Twitter to process and gain insights from vast amounts of tweets and user interactions in real time. This scalable architecture helps Twitter provide trending topics and analytics to its users.

6. Sony Pictures Imageworks: Rendering Visual Effects

SONY PICTURES IMAGEWORKS, a leader in visual effects and animation, relies on GCP for rendering complex scenes in movies like "Spider-Man: Into the Spider-Verse." GCP's Compute Engine and Cloud GPUs provide the computational power needed for rendering high-quality visual effects on tight deadlines.

7. DoorDash: Optimizing Food Delivery

DOORDASH, A FOOD DELIVERY platform, uses Google Cloud to optimize food delivery routes. Machine learning and Google Maps APIs help DoorDash determine the most efficient routes for its drivers, reducing delivery times and costs. Scalability ensures that the platform can handle increased demand during peak hours.

8. AirAsia: Enhancing Customer Experience

AIRASIA, A LEADING low-cost airline, leverages GCP to enhance its customer experience. By analyzing data from various sources, including social media and booking platforms, AirAsia gains insights into passenger preferences. This data-driven approach allows them to offer personalized services and improve overall satisfaction.

9. PayPal: Fraud Detection

PAYPAL, A GLOBAL ONLINE payment company, uses Google Cloud's machine learning and data analytics capabilities to detect and prevent fraudulent transactions. GCP enables PayPal to analyze vast amounts of transaction data in real time, identifying potential fraud patterns and protecting users' financial assets.

10. Netflix: Content Delivery

NETFLIX, A POPULAR streaming service, relies on GCP for content delivery and analytics. Google Cloud's Content Delivery Network (CDN) ensures fast and reliable streaming worldwide. Additionally, GCP analytics tools help Netflix understand user preferences and optimize content recommendations.

These case studies demonstrate the versatility of Google Cloud Platform in supporting diverse industries and applications. Whether it's handling massive user growth, analyzing real-time data, optimizing delivery routes, or rendering visual effects, GCP provides the scalability and tools needed to build successful and efficient solutions. Organizations of all sizes can benefit from GCP's cloud-native services to achieve their scalability and performance goals.

Chapter 12: Advanced Data Analytics

Section 12.1: Deep Dive into Data Analytics Services

IN THIS SECTION, WE will take a deep dive into the advanced data analytics services offered by Google Cloud Platform (GCP). Data analytics is a critical component for organizations aiming to extract valuable insights, make data-driven decisions, and gain a competitive edge. GCP provides a comprehensive suite of tools and services to meet the diverse needs of data analytics.

1. BigQuery: Data Warehousing and SQL Analytics

BIGQUERY IS GOOGLE Cloud's fully managed, serverless data warehouse. It is designed for super-fast SQL queries using the processing power of Google's infrastructure. BigQuery can handle massive datasets and allows you to run complex analytical queries. Its integration with Google Sheets and Data Studio makes it easy to visualize and share insights.

2. Dataflow: Real-Time Data Processing

GOOGLE CLOUD DATAFLOW is a fully managed, serverless stream and batch data processing service. It enables real-time data processing and analysis. You can build data pipelines to ingest, process, and transform data in real time. Dataflow is ideal for use cases like clickstream analysis, fraud detection, and IoT data processing.

3. Dataprep: Data Preparation and Cleaning

GOOGLE CLOUD DATAPREP is a visual data preparation tool that helps you clean, enrich, and transform your data without writing code. It provides a user-friendly interface for data wrangling tasks, making it accessible to data analysts and business users. Dataprep integrates seamlessly with other GCP services.

4. Data Studio: Data Visualization and Reporting

GOOGLE DATA STUDIO is a free data visualization tool that allows you to create interactive reports and dashboards. You can connect Data Studio to various data sources, including BigQuery and Google Sheets, to create compelling visualizations. It's a powerful tool for sharing insights across your organization.

5. Looker: Business Intelligence and Analytics Platform

LOOKER, NOW PART OF Google Cloud, is a modern business intelligence and data analytics platform. It provides a unified view of data and allows data exploration by non-technical users. Looker's modeling layer simplifies data access and ensures consistency in reporting and analysis.

6. AI and Machine Learning Integration

GCP'S DATA ANALYTICS services seamlessly integrate with AI and machine learning capabilities. You can leverage AI models built with AutoML or custom models using TensorFlow to gain deeper insights from your data. For example, you can perform sentiment analysis, image recognition, or demand forecasting.

7. Data Catalog: Data Discovery and Metadata Management

GOOGLE CLOUD DATA CATALOG is a fully managed and highly scalable metadata management service. It helps organizations discover and understand their data assets across GCP and beyond. Data Catalog provides a unified view of data lineage, schemas, and metadata.

8. Data Migration Services

GCP OFFERS VARIOUS data migration tools and services to help you move your data to the cloud seamlessly. Whether you are migrating databases, data warehouses, or unstructured data, Google Cloud provides solutions to simplify the process.

9. Data Lake and Storage Solutions

FOR ORGANIZATIONS DEALING with large volumes of unstructured or semi-structured data, GCP offers data lake and storage solutions like Cloud Storage and Cloud Bigtable. These services provide a scalable foundation for storing and processing diverse data types.

10. Managed Analytics: Beyond Infrastructure Management

ONE OF THE SIGNIFICANT advantages of using GCP's data analytics services is the managed aspect. Google Cloud takes care of infrastructure management, ensuring that you can focus on deriving insights from your data rather than worrying about hardware or software maintenance.

In this chapter, we will explore each of these data analytics services in more detail, including their features, use cases, and best practices. By the end of this chapter, you will have a comprehensive understanding of how to leverage Google Cloud Platform's advanced data analytics capabilities to drive data-driven decision-making in your organization.

Section 12.2: Streaming Analytics with Dataflow and Pub/Sub

IN THIS SECTION, WE will delve into streaming analytics using Google Cloud Dataflow and Cloud Pub/Sub. Streaming analytics is essential for processing and gaining insights from real-time data streams, making it valuable for applications like fraud detection, monitoring, and IoT data analysis.

1. Google Cloud Dataflow

GOOGLE CLOUD DATAFLOW is a powerful and fully managed stream and batch data processing service. It enables you to build data pipelines that can handle both real-time and batch data processing. Dataflow is based on the Apache Beam SDK, making it highly flexible and suitable for a wide range of streaming use cases.

To use Dataflow, you define your data processing logic using the Apache Beam SDK, which provides a unified programming model for both batch and stream processing. You can create data pipelines that read data from various sources, perform transformations, and write results to different sinks.

Here's a simple example of a Dataflow pipeline in Python that reads data from Pub/Sub, applies a transformation, and writes the results to BigQuery:

```
import apache_beam as beam
```

```
# Define a pipeline
with beam.Pipeline() as pipeline:
(
pipeline
| 'Read from Pub/Sub' >> beam.io.ReadFromPubSub(subscription='projects/<project-id>/subscripti
| 'Apply Transformation' >> beam.Map(lambda x: x.upper())
| 'Write to BigQuery' >> beam.io.WriteToBigQuery(
table='my-dataset.my-table',
schema='field:STRING',
write_disposition=beam.io.BigQueryDisposition.WRITE_APPEND,
create_disposition=beam.io.BigQueryDisposition.CREATE_IF_NEEDE
)
)
```

This pipeline reads messages from a Pub/Sub subscription, converts the text to uppercase, and stores the results in a BigQuery table.

2. Cloud Pub/Sub

CLOUD PUB/SUB IS A fully managed messaging service that allows you to build real-time, event-driven systems. It provides scalable and reliable message delivery, making it an excellent choice for ingesting streaming data.

To use Cloud Pub/Sub with Dataflow, you create a Pub/Sub topic and one or more subscriptions. Dataflow can then read messages from these subscriptions and process them in real time.

Here's how to create a Pub/Sub topic and subscription using the gcloud command-line tool:

```
# Create a Pub/Sub topic

gcloud pubsub topics create my-topic

# Create a subscription for the topic

gcloud pubsub subscriptions create my-subscription—topic=my-topic
```

Once you have a topic and subscription, you can publish messages to the topic, and Dataflow will automatically ingest and process them in your pipeline.

Streaming analytics with Dataflow and Pub/Sub is a robust solution for handling real-time data streams. It provides scalability, reliability, and the ability to build complex data processing pipelines for various use cases.

In the next section, we will explore data visualization with Looker and Data Studio, allowing you to create compelling visualizations and reports based on your analyzed data.

Section 12.3: Data Visualization with Looker and Data Studio

DATA VISUALIZATION is a crucial component of data analytics, as it allows you to present insights and patterns in a visually engaging and understandable way. Google Cloud Platform offers two powerful tools for data visualization: Looker and Data Studio.

1. Looker

LOOKER IS A DATA EXPLORATION and business intelligence platform that allows you to create and share interactive dashboards, reports, and data visualizations. It provides a user-friendly interface for exploring and analyzing data, making it an excellent choice for both technical and non-technical users.

Key features of Looker include:

- **Drag-and-Drop Interface**: Looker's interface is intuitive, enabling users to create reports and dashboards by simply dragging and dropping elements.
- **SQL-Based Queries**: Looker allows you to write SQL queries and then turn those queries into reusable data models and reports.
- **Collaboration**: Looker facilitates collaboration by allowing users to share and discuss reports within the platform.
- **Data Exploration**: Users can explore data and discover insights using interactive visualizations.
- **Data Governance**: Looker provides features for managing and controlling access to data, ensuring data governance and compliance.

Here's a basic example of Looker's LookML code, which defines a data model and explores data:

```
explore: orders {
from: orders
join: customers {
sql_on: ${orders.customer_id} = ${customers.id}
}
fields: {
order_date: date {
sql: ${TABLE}.created_at
type: time
}
total_amount: measure {
type: sum
sql: ${TABLE}.total_amount
}
}
}
```

With Looker, you can create customized dashboards and reports tailored to your business needs, helping you visualize and understand your data effectively.

2. Data Studio

GOOGLE DATA STUDIO is a free and cloud-based data visualization tool that allows you to create interactive and shareable reports and dashboards. It's designed to be user-friendly and accessible to individuals and teams without specialized technical skills.

Key features of Data Studio include:

- **Data Connectors**: Data Studio supports various data connectors, allowing you to pull data from different sources such as Google Analytics, BigQuery, Google Sheets, and more.

- **Drag-and-Drop Interface**: Similar to Looker, Data Studio offers a drag-and-drop interface for creating reports and dashboards.

- **Customizable Visualizations**: You can customize the appearance and style of your visualizations to match your brand or specific requirements.

- **Real-Time Data**: Data Studio can display real-time data, which is ideal for monitoring dashboards that require up-to-the-minute information.

- **Sharing and Collaboration**: Reports and dashboards created in Data Studio can be easily shared with collaborators, and you can control access and permissions.

Creating a report in Data Studio involves selecting a data source, adding charts and tables, customizing the design, and sharing the final report with others.

Both Looker and Data Studio offer powerful data visualization capabilities, and the choice between them depends on your specific requirements, budget, and familiarity with the tools. These tools play a crucial role in making data-driven decisions by turning raw data into actionable insights.

Section 12.4: Machine Learning in Big Data Analytics

MACHINE LEARNING (ML) is a transformative technology that has found numerous applications in big data analytics. Google Cloud Platform (GCP) offers a robust set of tools and services for integrating machine learning into your data analytics workflows. In this section, we'll explore how machine learning can enhance big data analytics on GCP.

1. BigQuery ML

BIGQUERY ML IS A FEATURE of Google BigQuery that allows users to create and execute machine learning models using SQL queries. It simplifies the process of building ML models by eliminating the need to move data to a separate ML service. You can use BigQuery ML to perform tasks such as regression, classification, and time series forecasting on your data directly within BigQuery.

Here's an example of creating a linear regression model using BigQuery ML:

```
CREATE OR REPLACE MODEL `project.dataset.model`

OPTIONS(model_type='linear_reg') AS

SELECT

feature1,
```

feature2,

target

FROM

`project.dataset.training_data`;

BigQuery ML handles the training, evaluation, and prediction steps, making it accessible to data analysts and engineers who are already familiar with SQL.

2. AI Platform

GOOGLE CLOUD AI PLATFORM provides a more comprehensive environment for developing, training, and deploying machine learning models. While it's not specific to big data analytics, AI Platform can be integrated with data stored in BigQuery, Cloud Storage, or other GCP services.

Key features of AI Platform include:

- **Custom Model Training**: You can use AI Platform to train custom machine learning models using frameworks like TensorFlow, scikit-learn, or XGBoost.
- **Hyperparameter Tuning**: AI Platform offers hyperparameter tuning to optimize model performance.
- **Online and Batch Prediction**: You can deploy models for both online (real-time) and batch (offline) predictions.
- **Model Versioning**: AI Platform allows you to manage multiple versions of your models, making it easy to iterate and deploy improvements.

3. AutoML

GOOGLE CLOUD AUTOML is designed for users who want to leverage machine learning without extensive expertise in the field. AutoML provides a suite of tools for tasks such as image classification, natural language processing, and tabular data prediction.

With AutoML, you can upload your data, and the service automatically trains and deploys a machine learning model. It's a powerful solution for tasks like sentiment analysis, object detection, and more.

4. Big Data and ML Integration

THE INTEGRATION OF big data and machine learning on GCP allows you to extract valuable insights from massive datasets. For example, you can use BigQuery to aggregate and preprocess data, then feed it into ML models for predictive analytics or anomaly detection.

Here's a simplified workflow:

1. **Data Ingestion**: Data is ingested into BigQuery from various sources, including IoT devices, logs, or external databases.
2. **Data Preparation**: BigQuery is used for data preprocessing, transformation, and feature engineering. This prepared data is then used for training ML models.
3. **Model Training**: ML models are trained using BigQuery ML, AI Platform, or AutoML, depending on the complexity of the task.
4. **Model Evaluation**: The trained models are evaluated to ensure they meet the desired performance criteria.

5. **Prediction and Analysis**: The models are used to make predictions on new data, uncover patterns, and gain insights.
6. **Visualization**: Data visualization tools like Looker or Data Studio can be used to create interactive reports and dashboards for presenting the results of big data analytics and machine learning.

Machine learning enhances big data analytics by automating decision-making, identifying hidden patterns, and improving the accuracy of predictions. By leveraging GCP's machine learning capabilities, organizations can extract more value from their big data investments and drive data-driven decision-making.

Section 12.5: Real-Time Analytics and Big Data Solutions

REAL-TIME ANALYTICS plays a crucial role in today's data-driven world. Organizations require up-to-the-minute insights to make informed decisions and respond rapidly to changing conditions. In this section, we'll explore real-time analytics solutions and their integration with big data on Google Cloud Platform (GCP).

1. Streaming Data on GCP

GCP OFFERS SEVERAL services for ingesting, processing, and analyzing streaming data. One of the core services for handling real-time data is **Cloud Pub/Sub**, a messaging service that allows you to publish and consume messages in real time. It serves as a bridge between data producers (e.g., IoT devices, application logs) and consumers (e.g., analytics pipelines, databases).

Here's how you can publish a message to a Cloud Pub/Sub topic using Python:

```
from google.cloud import pubsub_v1

publisher = pubsub_v1.PublisherClient()

topic_path = publisher.topic_path('your-project-id', 'your-topic-name')

data = "Your real-time data message".encode("utf-8")

future = publisher.publish(topic_path, data)

print(future.result())
```

Other GCP services like **Dataflow** and **Cloud Functions** can be used to process streaming data. Dataflow allows you to build data pipelines that can handle both batch and stream processing, while Cloud Functions enable you to execute code in response to events, making it suitable for real-time data processing.

2. Real-Time Analytics with BigQuery

BIGQUERY, GCP'S DATA warehousing and analytics service, provides real-time analytics capabilities. It allows you to run SQL queries on streaming data, making it possible to gain insights from data as it arrives.

To query streaming data in BigQuery, you need to create a table that references a streaming data source. Below is an example of creating a streaming table from a Pub/Sub topic:

```
CREATE OR REPLACE TABLE `your-project-id.your-dataset.your-table`

OPTIONS (
```

auto_create: **TRUE**,

time_partitioning: STRUCT(

type: "DAY",

field: "event_timestamp"

)

) **AS**

SELECT

TIMESTAMP_SECONDS(event_timestamp) **AS** event_timestamp,

FROM

`your-project-**id**.your-dataset.your-streaming-topic`

Once the streaming table is created, you can run SQL queries to perform real-time analytics on the incoming data.

3. Big Data and Real-Time Integration

REAL-TIME ANALYTICS is particularly valuable when combined with big data solutions. By processing streaming data and integrating it with historical data stored in big data repositories, organizations can gain comprehensive insights.

For instance, you can use Dataflow to join incoming streaming data with existing datasets in BigQuery or Cloud Storage. This enables you to perform real-time anomaly detection, fraud prevention, and customer personalization.

Additionally, **Data Studio** and **Looker** can be employed to create interactive dashboards and reports that visualize both real-time and batch data, providing a unified view of your analytics.

4. Use Cases

REAL-TIME ANALYTICS and big data integration have a wide range of use cases:

- **IoT Monitoring**: Monitor and analyze data from IoT devices in real time to detect anomalies, predict maintenance needs, and optimize operations.

- **Financial Services**: Detect fraudulent transactions as they happen, calculate risk in real time, and personalize financial offerings for customers.

- **E-commerce**: Provide real-time product recommendations based on user behavior, manage inventory, and track customer sentiment during shopping events.

- **Gaming**: Analyze player interactions in real time, optimize in-game experiences, and deliver personalized content.

In summary, real-time analytics and big data solutions on GCP enable organizations to harness the power of data as it flows into their systems. Whether you're dealing with IoT data, financial transactions, or user interactions, GCP provides the tools to process, analyze, and gain insights from streaming data in real time, helping you make data-driven decisions and stay competitive in today's fast-paced business environment.

Chapter 13: Internet of Things (IoT) on GCP

Section 13.1: Introduction to IoT in Cloud Computing

THE INTERNET OF THINGS (IoT) represents a paradigm shift in the way we interact with the physical world. It involves connecting everyday objects and devices to the internet, allowing them to collect and exchange data, and enabling remote control and automation. In this section, we'll explore the role of Google Cloud Platform (GCP) in facilitating IoT solutions and dive into the fundamentals of IoT in cloud computing.

1. IoT Fundamentals

IOT IS A BROAD FIELD encompassing various technologies, but it typically involves the following key components:

- **Devices and Sensors**: IoT devices are equipped with sensors and actuators to collect data and perform actions. These devices can range from simple temperature sensors to complex industrial machinery.

- **Connectivity**: IoT devices need to communicate with each other and with cloud services. This requires connectivity options such as Wi-Fi, cellular networks, or Low-Power Wide-Area Networks (LPWAN).

- **Data Processing**: The data generated by IoT devices can be massive and unstructured. Cloud platforms like GCP provide the infrastructure to ingest, process, and analyze this data at scale.

- **Applications**: IoT data is valuable when it can be translated into meaningful insights or actions. IoT applications and dashboards allow users to interact with and derive value from the data.

2. Why IoT in the Cloud?

CLOUD COMPUTING IS a natural fit for IoT for several reasons:

- **Scalability**: Cloud platforms can handle the rapid growth of IoT deployments. You can scale resources up or down as needed, ensuring that your infrastructure can accommodate millions of devices.

- **Data Processing**: IoT generates large volumes of data. Cloud services like BigQuery, Dataflow, and Pub/Sub can handle real-time data processing, analytics, and storage.

- **Security**: Cloud providers invest heavily in security, making it easier to implement robust security measures for IoT deployments, including device authentication, data encryption, and access control.

- **Global Reach**: Cloud providers have data centers worldwide, ensuring low-latency connectivity for IoT devices and users regardless of their location.

3. GCP IoT Core

GOOGLE CLOUD IOT CORE is a fully managed service that simplifies IoT device management. It provides features like device registration, telemetry ingestion, and command delivery. IoT Core can scale to support millions of devices and integrates seamlessly with other GCP services.

To get started with GCP IoT Core, you can create a registry for your devices and then register each device in that registry. Here's a high-level overview of the steps:

1. **Create a Registry**: Use the GCP Console or Cloud SDK to create an IoT Core registry, specifying the configuration options.
2. **Register Devices**: For each IoT device, you'll need to generate credentials and register the device with the IoT Core registry.
3. **Device Communication**: IoT devices can send telemetry data to IoT Core, which then forwards it to other GCP services for processing and analysis.
4. **Device Management**: IoT Core allows you to remotely manage and update device configurations and firmware.

4. IoT Use Cases

IOT IS APPLIED ACROSS various industries and use cases:

- **Smart Cities**: IoT sensors monitor traffic, control streetlights, and optimize waste management.

- **Healthcare**: Wearable devices track patient health, and medical equipment is remotely monitored for maintenance.

- **Manufacturing**: IoT devices in factories improve automation, predict equipment failures, and optimize production.

- **Agriculture**: Sensors monitor soil conditions, weather, and crop health for precision agriculture.

- **Retail**: Smart shelves track inventory, and beacons provide personalized shopping experiences.

In conclusion, IoT in cloud computing, especially on Google Cloud Platform, offers a robust and scalable solution for managing and deriving insights from IoT devices. With GCP IoT Core and other services, organizations can harness the potential of IoT to optimize operations, enhance customer experiences, and drive innovation across various industries.

Section 13.2: GCP's IoT Core: Features and Capabilities

GOOGLE CLOUD PLATFORM'S (GCP) IoT Core is a powerful and fully managed service designed to simplify the management and operation of IoT devices at scale. In this section, we'll delve into the features and capabilities of GCP's IoT Core, highlighting how it enables organizations to effectively manage their IoT deployments.

1. Device Registry

ONE OF THE CORE COMPONENTS of IoT Core is the Device Registry. It serves as a container for managing devices with similar characteristics. You can create multiple registries for different device types or groups, making it easier to organize and manage your IoT fleet. Each device within a registry is identified by a unique device ID.

2. Device Authentication and Security

IOT CORE PLACES A STRONG emphasis on security. Devices connecting to IoT Core must use strong, device-specific credentials for authentication. This ensures that only authorized devices can communicate with your IoT Core instance. Additionally, data transmitted between devices and IoT Core is encrypted to protect it from interception.

3. Telemetry Data Ingestion

IOT DEVICES GENERATE telemetry data, which may include sensor readings, status updates, or other information. IoT Core provides a robust and scalable infrastructure for ingesting this telemetry data. Devices can send data to IoT Core using various protocols like MQTT or HTTP.

4. Command Delivery

IOT CORE ENABLES TWO-way communication between the cloud and devices. You can send commands to devices from the cloud, allowing you to remotely control and configure them. This feature is valuable for scenarios where device behavior needs to be modified in real-time.

5. Device State Management

IOT CORE KEEPS TRACK of the state of each device, allowing you to monitor their status and health. You can query the state of devices and trigger actions based on their state changes. This feature is crucial for proactive maintenance and troubleshooting.

6. Scaling and Performance

IOT CORE IS DESIGNED to scale horizontally, accommodating IoT deployments of all sizes, from small prototypes to massive industrial deployments. It can handle millions of devices and messages per second, ensuring high performance and reliability.

7. Integration with GCP Services

ONE OF THE STRENGTHS of IoT Core is its seamless integration with other GCP services. You can easily connect IoT Core to services like Pub/Sub, Dataflow, BigQuery, and more. This integration enables real-time data processing, analytics, and visualization of IoT data.

8. Device Management

MANAGING IOT DEVICES can be challenging, especially when you have a large fleet. IoT Core simplifies device management by providing tools for updating device configurations and firmware over-the-air (OTA). This feature is essential for keeping devices up-to-date and secure.

9. Role-Based Access Control (RBAC)

IOT CORE SUPPORTS ROLE-Based Access Control, allowing you to define fine-grained permissions and access control policies. This ensures that only authorized personnel can interact with your IoT deployment and data.

10. Event Triggering

YOU CAN SET UP EVENT triggers in IoT Core to automate actions based on incoming data or device state changes. For example, you can trigger alerts or initiate workflows when specific conditions are met.

11. Device Simulation and Testing

IOT CORE PROVIDES TOOLS for simulating device behavior and testing your IoT applications at scale. This is invaluable during the development and testing phases of an IoT project.

12. Pricing Model

IOT CORE OFFERS A PRICING model based on the number of devices and the volume of data ingested and egressed. It's essential to understand the pricing structure to effectively manage costs, especially for large-scale deployments.

In summary, Google Cloud Platform's IoT Core is a comprehensive solution for managing IoT devices and data at scale. Its rich set of features, security measures, and integration with other GCP services make it a valuable choice for organizations looking to harness the power of IoT in the cloud. Whether you're building a smart city infrastructure, monitoring industrial equipment, or enabling new consumer experiences, IoT Core provides the tools and capabilities you need to succeed.

Section 13.3: Building IoT Solutions with GCP

BUILDING IOT SOLUTIONS with Google Cloud Platform (GCP) involves a combination of services and tools that enable you to create, deploy, and manage IoT applications. In this section, we'll explore the key steps and considerations for building IoT solutions using GCP.

1. Define Your Use Case

BEFORE DIVING INTO the technical aspects, it's essential to define your IoT use case. What problem are you trying to solve with IoT? Are you monitoring equipment, tracking assets, or collecting sensor data for analysis? Clarifying your use case helps you choose the right IoT devices, sensors, and data processing pipelines.

2. Choose IoT Devices and Sensors

SELECTING THE APPROPRIATE IoT devices and sensors is crucial. GCP supports a wide range of devices, from microcontrollers and single-board computers to industrial sensors. Consider factors like connectivity (Wi-Fi, cellular, LoRaWAN), power requirements, and environmental conditions when choosing devices.

3. Connect Devices to IoT Core

GOOGLE CLOUD IOT CORE is the central component for connecting and managing IoT devices. You'll need to create a device registry for your devices and configure device authentication. IoT Core supports popular IoT protocols like MQTT and HTTP, making it easy to connect devices securely.

4. Ingest Data into Cloud Storage

ONCE DATA IS GENERATED by your IoT devices, you'll want to ingest it into GCP for processing and analysis. Google Cloud Storage is an excellent option for storing raw IoT data. You can use Cloud Storage buckets to organize data by device type, location, or other criteria.

5. Real-Time Data Processing with Cloud Pub/Sub

FOR REAL-TIME DATA processing and analysis, Cloud Pub/Sub is a powerful service. It allows you to ingest streaming data and publish it to other GCP services, such as Dataflow, BigQuery, or Cloud Functions. Pub/Sub can handle high-throughput data streams from IoT devices.

6. Data Transformation with Dataflow

GOOGLE CLOUD DATAFLOW provides a way to process, transform, and enrich IoT data streams in real-time. You can create data pipelines using Dataflow to clean, aggregate, or enrich data before it's stored or analyzed. This is particularly useful for data normalization and quality control.

7. Analyze Data with BigQuery

BIGQUERY IS GCP'S SERVERLESS, scalable data warehouse that can handle large volumes of IoT data. You can use SQL queries to analyze historical data, identify trends, and gain insights. BigQuery ML also enables machine learning models to be trained directly on IoT data.

8. Visualize Data with Data Studio and Looker

TO MAKE SENSE OF YOUR IoT data, consider using data visualization tools like Data Studio and Looker. These tools allow you to create interactive dashboards and reports to monitor device performance, track KPIs, and make data-driven decisions.

9. Alerting and Monitoring

GCP OFFERS MONITORING and alerting capabilities through Cloud Monitoring and Cloud Logging. You can set up custom alerts to be notified of critical events or anomalies in your IoT data, ensuring proactive issue resolution.

10. Device Management and Updates

MANAGING IOT DEVICES at scale involves device configuration, firmware updates, and remote management. Google

Cloud IoT Core provides features for managing devices, including over-the-air (OTA) updates and remote device control.

11. Scalability and Security

AS YOUR IOT DEPLOYMENT grows, ensure that your architecture is scalable and secure. GCP provides tools and best practices for securing IoT data, implementing identity and access management, and scaling your infrastructure to handle more devices and data.

12. Cost Optimization

OPTIMIZING COSTS IS essential, especially in large-scale IoT deployments. Take advantage of GCP's pricing models, which include free tier usage and cost-effective data storage options, to manage your IoT project's expenses effectively.

In conclusion, building IoT solutions with Google Cloud Platform offers a robust and scalable ecosystem of services and tools. By following these steps and considering your specific use case, you can leverage GCP's capabilities to create powerful IoT applications that drive business value and innovation.

Section 13.4: Analyzing IoT Data in the Cloud

ONCE YOU'VE COLLECTED data from your Internet of Things (IoT) devices and ingested it into Google Cloud Platform (GCP), the next step is to analyze this data to derive valuable insights. In this section, we'll explore the process of analyzing IoT data in the cloud.

1. Data Preprocessing

BEFORE DIVING INTO data analysis, it's often necessary to preprocess the IoT data. This step involves cleaning, transforming, and structuring the data for analysis. You may need to handle missing values, convert data types, and ensure data consistency. Google Cloud Dataflow can be a valuable tool for real-time data preprocessing.

2. Real-Time Data Streaming

IOT DATA IS TYPICALLY generated continuously in real time. To handle this stream of data, use Google Cloud Pub/Sub. It enables you to ingest, process, and route data streams from IoT devices to various GCP services seamlessly.

3. Data Storage

FOR HISTORICAL DATA storage and easy retrieval, Google Cloud Bigtable and Google Cloud BigQuery are excellent choices. Bigtable is a NoSQL database designed for high-throughput and low-latency data storage, while BigQuery is a fully managed data warehouse optimized for large-scale data analysis.

4. Data Analysis Tools

GCP PROVIDES A VARIETY of tools for data analysis, including Google Data Studio, Google Looker, and Jupyter notebooks. Data Studio and Looker allow you to create interactive dashboards and reports to visualize IoT data trends and insights. Jupyter notebooks can be used for more advanced data analysis and machine learning tasks.

5. Machine Learning and AI

TO EXTRACT DEEPER INSIGHTS from your IoT data, consider leveraging machine learning and artificial intelligence (AI). Google Cloud AI Platform offers a range of services for building, training, and deploying machine learning models. You can use historical IoT data to train models for predictive maintenance, anomaly detection, or forecasting.

6. Real-Time Monitoring and Alerts

TO MONITOR IOT DATA and receive alerts for critical events or anomalies, utilize Google Cloud Monitoring and Cloud Logging. These services enable you to set up custom alerting rules and gain real-time visibility into your IoT infrastructure's health and performance.

7. Data Security and Compliance

IOT DATA OFTEN CONTAINS sensitive information, making data security a top priority. Ensure that you implement robust security measures, including encryption, identity and access management (IAM), and compliance with relevant regulations, such as GDPR or HIPAA, if applicable to your use case.

8. Scalability and Performance

AS YOUR IOT DEPLOYMENT grows, ensure that your data analysis pipelines are scalable and performant. GCP's serverless architecture allows you to scale resources dynamically to handle increasing data volumes.

9. Cost Optimization

OPTIMIZING COSTS IS crucial when dealing with IoT data, especially as data volumes increase. GCP offers cost-effective storage solutions, tiered storage, and pricing models that help you manage your data analysis expenses efficiently.

10. Iterative Analysis and Improvement

IOT DATA ANALYSIS IS an iterative process. Continuously refine your analysis techniques and models based on the insights gained. Regularly assess the accuracy of predictions and the effectiveness of your monitoring and alerting systems.

In conclusion, analyzing IoT data in the cloud with Google Cloud Platform empowers organizations to make data-driven decisions, optimize operations, and gain a competitive edge. By following best practices and leveraging GCP's powerful data analytics tools, you can extract valuable insights from your IoT data to drive business success.

Section 13.5: Case Studies: IoT Implementations Using GCP

IN THIS SECTION, WE'LL explore real-world case studies of Internet of Things (IoT) implementations using Google Cloud Platform (GCP). These examples demonstrate how organizations have leveraged GCP's IoT capabilities to address specific business challenges and achieve remarkable results.

1. Smart Manufacturing

A GLOBAL MANUFACTURING company adopted GCP's IoT Core to connect and monitor machines across its factories. By collecting real-time data from sensors and machines, they gained insights into production efficiency, equipment health, and quality control. Predictive maintenance models were deployed using Google Cloud AI to reduce downtime and improve machine reliability. This resulted in a 20% reduction in maintenance costs and a 15% increase in overall equipment effectiveness.

2. Precision Agriculture

AN AGRICULTURAL COOPERATIVE implemented an IoT solution with GCP to optimize farming practices. Soil moisture sensors, weather stations, and GPS trackers were used to collect data from fields. GCP's data analytics tools were employed to analyze this data, enabling farmers to make data-driven decisions on irrigation, planting schedules, and crop yield optimization. As a result, water usage decreased by 30%, and crop yields increased by 15%.

3. Healthcare and Remote Patient Monitoring

A HEALTHCARE PROVIDER utilized GCP's IoT capabilities to develop a remote patient monitoring system. Patients with chronic illnesses were equipped with wearable IoT devices that transmitted vital signs and health data to GCP. Machine learning models on Google Cloud AI Platform were used to predict health deteriorations and trigger timely interventions. This reduced hospital readmissions by 25% and improved patient outcomes.

4. Logistics and Fleet Management

A LOGISTICS COMPANY integrated GCP's IoT solutions to track and optimize its fleet of vehicles. GPS trackers, temperature sensors, and vehicle telematics data were collected in real time. Google Cloud Pub/Sub and BigQuery enabled real-time tracking and route optimization. The company achieved a 15% reduction in fuel consumption, lower maintenance costs, and improved delivery timelines.

5. Energy Management

A UTILITY COMPANY DEPLOYED IoT devices across its power distribution infrastructure to monitor grid health and manage energy consumption efficiently. GCP's data analytics and machine learning tools were used to analyze sensor data and predict grid failures. This proactive approach reduced unplanned outages by 40%, saved operational costs, and improved grid reliability.

6. Retail Inventory Management

A RETAIL CHAIN IMPLEMENTED GCP's IoT solutions to enhance inventory management. RFID sensors and IoT devices were used to track inventory levels in real time. The data was processed and analyzed with Google Cloud Dataflow and BigQuery, providing insights into stock levels, demand patterns, and inventory turnover. This led to a 20% reduction in stockouts, optimized inventory carrying costs, and improved customer satisfaction.

7. Environmental Monitoring

AN ENVIRONMENTAL AGENCY leveraged GCP's IoT capabilities to monitor air quality in urban areas. Sensors placed throughout the city collected data on pollutants, temperature, and humidity. GCP's data analytics and visualization tools helped create real-time air quality maps accessible to the public. This initiative led to increased awareness of air quality issues and better-informed decisions to reduce pollution.

8. Smart Buildings

A PROPERTY MANAGEMENT company adopted GCP's IoT solutions to create smart buildings. IoT sensors were used for occupancy detection, temperature control, and energy management. GCP's machine learning models analyzed data to optimize heating, ventilation, and air conditioning (HVAC) systems. This resulted in energy savings of up to 30% and improved tenant comfort.

These case studies demonstrate the versatility and effectiveness of Google Cloud Platform in addressing a wide range of IoT use cases. By harnessing the power of GCP's IoT capabilities, organizations can drive innovation, improve operational efficiency, and deliver valuable services to their customers.

Chapter 14: Hybrid and Multi-Cloud Environments

Section 14.1: The Rise of Hybrid and Multi-Cloud Strategies

IN RECENT YEARS, THERE has been a significant shift in how organizations approach cloud computing. The rise of hybrid and multi-cloud strategies has fundamentally changed the way businesses think about their IT infrastructure and cloud adoption. In this section, we will explore the concepts and benefits of hybrid and multi-cloud environments.

Understanding Hybrid Cloud

A HYBRID CLOUD IS AN IT architecture that combines on-premises infrastructure (often referred to as the "private cloud") with public cloud resources. This approach allows organizations to leverage the scalability and flexibility of the public cloud while maintaining control over sensitive data and critical workloads within their private data centers.

Hybrid clouds offer several advantages, including:

- **Flexibility:** Organizations can scale resources up or down as needed, making it easier to handle fluctuations in demand.

- **Cost Efficiency:** Hybrid models can optimize costs by using public cloud resources for non-sensitive workloads and reserving private infrastructure for mission-critical tasks.

- **Data Security:** Sensitive data can be kept on-premises, reducing the risk of exposure to external threats.

- **Compliance:** Hybrid setups enable compliance with industry-specific regulations that require data to be stored in specific locations or under certain conditions.

Embracing Multi-Cloud

MULTI-CLOUD TAKES THE concept of hybrid cloud a step further by incorporating multiple public cloud providers into the mix. Instead of relying on a single cloud vendor, organizations use a combination of services from different providers, such as Google Cloud Platform (GCP), Amazon Web Services (AWS), and Microsoft Azure.

Key benefits of a multi-cloud strategy include:

- **Reduced Vendor Lock-In:** With multi-cloud, organizations are not tied to a single cloud provider, giving them more negotiating power and flexibility.

- **Best-of-Breed Services:** Organizations can choose the best services from each cloud provider to meet specific requirements.

- **Disaster Recovery:** Multi-cloud setups enhance disaster recovery capabilities by ensuring data redundancy across different cloud platforms.

- **Geographic Diversity:** Data and services can be distributed across multiple regions or data centers for improved latency and availability.

Use Cases for Hybrid and Multi-Cloud

THE ADOPTION OF HYBRID and multi-cloud strategies is driven by various use cases:

1. **High Availability:** Businesses that require 24/7 availability leverage hybrid and multi-cloud architectures to minimize downtime.
2. **Global Reach:** Organizations with a global presence can use multi-cloud to host services in regions closest to their customers, reducing latency.
3. **Scalability:** Hybrid and multi-cloud environments make it easier to scale resources on-demand to accommodate traffic spikes.
4. **Data Governance:** Companies subject to data sovereignty laws benefit from hybrid clouds, which allow them to store data in specific geographic locations.
5. **Cost Optimization:** Multi-cloud strategies enable cost optimization by choosing the most cost-effective cloud services for specific workloads.
6. **Disaster Recovery:** Hybrid and multi-cloud setups enhance disaster recovery and business continuity planning by providing redundancy across multiple clouds.

Challenges and Considerations

WHILE HYBRID AND MULTI-cloud strategies offer numerous advantages, they also introduce challenges. Organizations must consider factors like data integration, security, compliance, and the complexity of managing multiple cloud providers. However, with careful planning and the right tools, businesses can harness the full potential of these innovative cloud computing approaches.

In the following sections of this chapter, we will delve deeper into the tools and techniques for implementing and managing hybrid and multi-cloud environments effectively.

Section 14.2: Anthos: Google's Hybrid and Multi-Cloud Platform

GOOGLE'S ANTHOS IS a powerful platform designed to simplify the management and operation of applications across hybrid and multi-cloud environments. Anthos enables organizations to build, deploy, and manage applications consistently across on-premises data centers, Google Cloud Platform (GCP), and other cloud providers. In this section, we'll explore the key features and benefits of Anthos.

Key Features of Anthos

ANTHOS PROVIDES A COMPREHENSIVE set of features and capabilities that make it a compelling solution for hybrid and multi-cloud management:

1. **Hybrid and Multi-Cloud Kubernetes:** Anthos leverages Kubernetes as its orchestration platform, enabling consistent containerized application deployment across different environments. This uniformity simplifies operations and reduces the risk of vendor lock-in.
2. **Managed Kubernetes (GKE On-Prem):** Anthos includes GKE On-Prem, a managed Kubernetes service that allows organizations to run Kubernetes clusters on their own data center infrastructure. Google manages the control plane, ensuring security and reliability.
3. **Anthos Config Management:** This feature provides policy and configuration management for Kubernetes clusters

across multiple environments. It allows administrators to define and enforce policies consistently, ensuring compliance and security.

4. **Application Modernization:** Anthos facilitates the modernization of legacy applications by containerizing them and making them Kubernetes-ready. This approach enables organizations to benefit from cloud-native architectures.
5. **Service Mesh with Istio:** Anthos integrates with Istio, an open-source service mesh platform. Istio provides features like traffic management, security, and observability, enhancing the reliability of applications in a microservices environment.
6. **Anthos Service Mesh:** This service extends Istio to provide a unified and secure service mesh across hybrid and multi-cloud environments. It simplifies service-to-service communication, improves visibility, and enhances security.
7. **Anthos Security:** Anthos offers a range of security features, including identity and access management (IAM), binary authorization, and vulnerability scanning. These tools help organizations maintain a strong security posture in their hybrid and multi-cloud deployments.

Benefits of Anthos

ANTHOS OFFERS SEVERAL advantages to organizations embracing hybrid and multi-cloud strategies:

- **Portability:** Applications can be developed and tested in one environment and seamlessly deployed in another, reducing development time and ensuring consistency.

- **Scalability:** Anthos simplifies scaling applications horizontally and vertically across different environments, ensuring optimal resource utilization.

- **Security and Compliance:** With Anthos, organizations can enforce consistent security policies and compliance standards across all environments, reducing security risks.

- **Visibility and Monitoring:** Anthos provides centralized visibility and monitoring tools, making it easier to troubleshoot issues and ensure the health of applications.

- **Cost Management:** Anthos helps organizations optimize cloud spending by providing insights into resource usage and recommendations for cost reduction.

Use Cases for Anthos

ANTHOS IS WELL-SUITED for various use cases, including:

1. **Modernizing Legacy Applications:** Organizations can use Anthos to containerize and modernize legacy applications, making them cloud-ready and more scalable.
2. **Multi-Cloud and Hybrid Cloud Management:** Anthos simplifies the management of applications running in hybrid and multi-cloud environments, reducing complexity and improving efficiency.
3. **Application Portability:** Anthos enables applications to run consistently across different cloud providers, providing flexibility and avoiding vendor lock-in.
4. **Security and Compliance:** Anthos helps organizations enforce security and compliance policies consistently

across all environments, ensuring data protection and regulatory compliance.

5. **Edge Computing:** Anthos can extend applications to the edge, enabling low-latency processing for IoT and other edge use cases.

In the following sections, we will explore how to deploy and manage applications using Anthos and best practices for implementing hybrid and multi-cloud strategies effectively.

Section 14.3: Integrating On-Premises with GCP

INTEGRATING ON-PREMISES data centers with Google Cloud Platform (GCP) is a crucial aspect of hybrid cloud and multi-cloud strategies. This integration allows organizations to leverage the scalability, flexibility, and services of the cloud while still utilizing their existing on-premises infrastructure. In this section, we'll explore the key considerations and methods for integrating on-premises environments with GCP.

Key Considerations for Integration

BEFORE EMBARKING ON an on-premises integration with GCP, several key considerations should be taken into account:

1. **Network Connectivity:** Establishing a reliable and secure network connection between your on-premises data center and GCP is fundamental. Google Cloud Interconnect and VPN options are available to facilitate this connection.
2. **Data Transfer:** Consider how data will be transferred between on-premises and GCP. Tools like Cloud Data Transfer Service and Storage Transfer Service can simplify

data migration.

3. **Identity and Access Management (IAM):** Implement a consistent IAM strategy that spans both on-premises and cloud environments. Google's Identity-Aware Proxy (IAP) can help manage access securely.
4. **Security and Compliance:** Ensure that security and compliance policies are consistent across both environments. Use tools like Google Cloud's Security Command Center to monitor and enforce security policies.
5. **Hybrid Identity Management:** If your organization uses Active Directory, consider integrating it with GCP using Cloud Identity-Aware Proxy (Cloud IAP) or Cloud Directory Sync (GCDS).

Integration Methods

SEVERAL METHODS AND technologies can be employed to integrate on-premises environments with GCP:

1. **Cloud VPN:** Google Cloud VPN allows you to establish a secure IPsec connection between your on-premises network and GCP. This method is suitable for low to moderate data transfer needs.
2. **Cloud Interconnect:** Google Cloud Interconnect provides dedicated, high-bandwidth connections between your on-premises data center and Google's network edge. It offers more reliability and performance compared to VPN connections.
3. **Direct Peering:** Direct Peering is a Google service that enables direct network peering between your on-premises network and GCP. It allows for lower latency and improved performance.

4. **Data Transfer Services:** Google Cloud provides services like Cloud Data Transfer Service and Storage Transfer Service to facilitate data migration between on-premises and cloud environments. These services simplify the process of transferring large volumes of data.

Use Cases for On-Premises Integration

INTEGRATING ON-PREMISES environments with GCP can address various use cases:

1. **Data Backup and Recovery:** Organizations can use GCP for data backup and disaster recovery (DR) by replicating on-premises data to the cloud. In case of a disaster, data can be quickly restored from GCP.
2. **Hybrid Applications:** Applications can be designed to run in a hybrid fashion, with some components on-premises and others in GCP. This allows for flexibility and scalability.
3. **Data Analytics:** Organizations can leverage GCP's data analytics and machine learning services to gain insights from on-premises data without the need for significant data migration.
4. **Bursting Workloads:** During peak demand, organizations can offload workloads to GCP to handle the increased load, ensuring optimal performance without over-provisioning on-premises infrastructure.
5. **Edge Computing:** Integrating GCP with edge devices and sensors enables real-time data processing and analysis at the edge, suitable for IoT and edge computing scenarios.

In the following sections, we will delve deeper into the technical aspects of on-premises integration with GCP, providing guidance on implementing these solutions effectively.

Section 14.4: Managing Multi-Cloud Environments with GCP

MANAGING MULTI-CLOUD environments, where an organization utilizes services and resources from multiple cloud providers, can be a complex task. Google Cloud Platform (GCP) offers tools and services to help organizations effectively manage their multi-cloud deployments, ensuring seamless operation and optimization across various cloud providers.

Challenges of Multi-Cloud Management

MANAGING MULTI-CLOUD environments poses several challenges:

1. **Vendor Lock-In:** Organizations may want to avoid vendor lock-in by distributing workloads across multiple cloud providers. This approach allows them to choose the best services from each provider.
2. **Complexity:** Managing resources, applications, and data across different cloud providers can be complex and require expertise in each provider's services.
3. **Cost Management:** Tracking and optimizing costs across multiple providers can be challenging, leading to cost overruns.
4. **Security and Compliance:** Ensuring consistent security and compliance policies across different clouds can be a significant concern.

Google Cloud's Multi-Cloud Management Solutions

GCP PROVIDES SOLUTIONS to address these challenges:

1. **Anthos:** Anthos is Google's multi-cloud platform that allows you to manage and deploy applications across GCP, on-premises, and other cloud providers, such as AWS and Azure. It provides a consistent platform and enables workload portability.
2. **Apigee:** Apigee, a Google Cloud service, helps manage APIs across multiple cloud providers. It provides API analytics, security, and developer portal capabilities for API management.
3. **Cloud Asset Inventory:** Google Cloud's Cloud Asset Inventory allows you to discover and manage assets across different cloud providers. It provides visibility into resources, making it easier to track and manage them.
4. **Cost Management Tools:** Google Cloud offers cost management tools, such as Cost Explorer and Billing Reports, to help organizations monitor and optimize spending across multiple cloud providers.
5. **Security and Compliance:** Google Cloud provides security and compliance services, such as Cloud Security Command Center and Policy Advisor, to help organizations maintain consistent security and compliance policies across multi-cloud environments.

Use Cases for Multi-Cloud Management

MULTI-CLOUD MANAGEMENT is beneficial for various use cases:

1. **Disaster Recovery:** Organizations can use multi-cloud environments for disaster recovery, ensuring that critical

workloads can failover to a different cloud provider in case of a catastrophic event.

2. **Avoiding Downtime:** Multi-cloud setups can reduce the risk of downtime by spreading workloads across different cloud providers, minimizing the impact of provider-specific outages.
3. **Optimizing Costs:** Organizations can take advantage of cost disparities between cloud providers, optimizing expenses by choosing the most cost-effective services for specific workloads.
4. **Regulatory Compliance:** Multi-cloud deployments enable organizations to meet regulatory requirements by storing data in specific regions or using compliant services from different providers.
5. **Hybrid Cloud:** Combining on-premises, GCP, and other cloud providers in a hybrid setup allows organizations to create a flexible and scalable environment.

In conclusion, managing multi-cloud environments with GCP's tools and services can help organizations overcome the challenges of multi-cloud deployments, achieve cost optimization, and maintain consistent security and compliance policies across diverse cloud providers. It provides the flexibility needed to build resilient and efficient cloud infrastructures.

Section 14.5: Security and Compliance in Hybrid and Multi-Cloud Systems

SECURITY AND COMPLIANCE are paramount concerns when managing hybrid and multi-cloud environments. Ensuring that data and applications are protected, and regulatory requirements are met across diverse cloud and on-premises infrastructures is a complex but crucial task.

Challenges in Security and Compliance

1. **Diverse Environments:** Hybrid and multi-cloud setups involve a mix of on-premises data centers and cloud providers, each with its own security mechanisms and tools.
2. **Data Protection:** Sensitive data must be safeguarded during transit and at rest. Encryption, access controls, and data classification are essential.
3. **Identity and Access Management (IAM):** Managing user access and permissions consistently across different environments can be challenging.
4. **Compliance Requirements:** Meeting industry-specific regulations and standards, such as GDPR or HIPAA, across hybrid and multi-cloud environments requires careful planning and monitoring.

Security Best Practices

TO ADDRESS THESE CHALLENGES, consider the following security best practices:

1. **Zero Trust Security Model:** Implement a zero-trust security model, where trust is never assumed and verification is required from anyone trying to access resources in your environment.
2. **Identity Federation:** Use identity federation solutions to provide a unified authentication and authorization mechanism across different cloud providers and on-premises systems.

3. **Encryption:** Encrypt data both in transit and at rest. Leverage cloud-native encryption services and key management solutions.
4. **Security Automation:** Implement security automation and continuous monitoring to detect and respond to threats promptly.
5. **Access Control:** Define and enforce access controls consistently. Utilize role-based access control (RBAC) and fine-grained permissions.
6. **Security Information and Event Management (SIEM):** Use SIEM solutions to centralize security logs and events from various sources for analysis and alerting.

Compliance Considerations

1. **Data Classification:** Classify data based on its sensitivity to apply appropriate security measures and access controls.
2. **Audit and Logging:** Enable auditing and logging for all relevant resources and services. Retain logs for compliance reporting.
3. **Compliance Tools:** Leverage compliance and governance tools provided by your cloud provider to assist in meeting regulatory requirements.
4. **Regular Assessments:** Conduct regular security and compliance assessments to identify and rectify vulnerabilities or non-compliance issues.
5. **Documentation:** Maintain documentation of security controls and compliance measures for auditing purposes.

Case Study: Achieving Compliance in a Hybrid Environment

CONSIDER A HEALTHCARE organization operating a hybrid cloud environment. They must comply with the Health Insurance Portability and Accountability Act (HIPAA). To achieve compliance:

- The organization encrypts patient data in transit and at rest using cloud-native encryption services.

- Identity federation is implemented to ensure consistent access controls across on-premises systems and cloud resources.

- Regular vulnerability assessments and penetration testing are conducted to identify and mitigate security risks.

- Auditing and logging are enabled for all healthcare-related data and services, with logs retained as per HIPAA requirements.

- Security policies and compliance documentation are maintained and regularly updated.

By following these security and compliance best practices, the healthcare organization can maintain the security of patient data and meet the stringent requirements of HIPAA in its hybrid cloud environment.

In conclusion, security and compliance in hybrid and multi-cloud environments require a combination of robust security practices, identity management, encryption, and adherence to regulatory standards. Organizations must continually assess and adapt their security measures to mitigate risks effectively and ensure compliance with relevant regulations.

Chapter 15: Disaster Recovery and Business Continuity

Section 15.1: Understanding Disaster Recovery in the Cloud

DISASTER RECOVERY (DR) is a critical component of any organization's IT strategy. It involves preparing for and recovering from events that could disrupt normal business operations. These events can range from natural disasters like earthquakes and hurricanes to human-made incidents like cyberattacks or hardware failures.

Challenges in Traditional Disaster Recovery

TRADITIONAL DISASTER recovery solutions often involve maintaining secondary data centers or backup facilities that mirror the primary infrastructure. While effective, these solutions have several challenges:

1. **High Costs:** Setting up and maintaining secondary data centers can be prohibitively expensive.
2. **Complexity:** Managing and synchronizing data between primary and secondary sites can be complex and error-prone.
3. **Resource Intensive:** Maintaining idle resources for potential disasters can lead to underutilization and increased costs.
4. **Limited Scalability:** Scaling traditional DR solutions can be slow and expensive.

Cloud-Based Disaster Recovery

CLOUD COMPUTING HAS transformed disaster recovery by offering cost-effective and scalable solutions. Here are key aspects to consider:

1. **Data Replication:** Cloud providers offer robust data replication mechanisms, allowing you to replicate your data to multiple geographically distributed data centers. This redundancy minimizes data loss during disasters.
2. **Scalability:** Cloud resources can be quickly scaled up or down based on demand. You pay only for the resources you use, making it cost-effective.
3. **Automation:** Disaster recovery processes can be automated in the cloud, ensuring rapid response during emergencies.
4. **Managed Services:** Cloud providers offer managed DR services, simplifying setup and maintenance.

Types of Cloud-Based Disaster Recovery

THERE ARE TWO PRIMARY approaches to cloud-based disaster recovery:

1. **Backup and Restore:** In this approach, backups of data and systems are stored in the cloud. In case of a disaster, data and systems can be restored from these backups. This is suitable for less critical workloads.
2. **Pilot Light:** In the pilot light approach, a minimal version of your infrastructure is continually running in the cloud. When a disaster occurs, the infrastructure can be quickly scaled up to support critical workloads. This approach is suitable for mission-critical applications.

Key Considerations for Cloud Disaster Recovery

WHEN IMPLEMENTING CLOUD-based disaster recovery, consider the following factors:

1. **Recovery Time Objective (RTO):** Define how quickly your systems need to be recovered after a disaster. The cloud provider's capabilities and your application's design impact this.
2. **Recovery Point Objective (RPO):** Determine how much data loss is acceptable. Regularly scheduled backups and data replication influence this metric.
3. **Testing:** Regularly test your disaster recovery plan to ensure it works as expected.
4. **Security:** Ensure that data replicated to the cloud is encrypted both in transit and at rest.
5. **Cost Management:** Understand the costs associated with cloud-based DR and optimize resource allocation.

Case Study: Cloud-Based Disaster Recovery in Action

CONSIDER AN E-COMMERCE company that relies heavily on its online platform. By using a cloud-based disaster recovery solution, they ensure that their website and customer data are replicated to a geographically separate data center maintained by their cloud provider.

In the event of a data center outage due to a natural disaster, the company can quickly redirect traffic to the replicated environment, minimizing downtime and data loss. This ensures continuity of their online business operations.

In conclusion, cloud-based disaster recovery offers organizations an efficient and cost-effective way to protect their data and applications from disasters. By leveraging cloud resources, organizations can improve their recovery capabilities, minimize downtime, and ensure business continuity in the face of unforeseen events.

Section 15.2: Designing a Disaster Recovery Plan on GCP

DESIGNING A DISASTER recovery (DR) plan on Google Cloud Platform (GCP) is essential to ensure business continuity and data resilience. GCP offers a robust set of tools and services to help organizations create effective DR strategies. In this section, we will explore the key steps and considerations when designing a DR plan on GCP.

1. Assessing Your Requirements

THE FIRST STEP IN CREATING a DR plan is to assess your organization's specific requirements. Consider the following factors:

- **RPO and RTO:** Determine your Recovery Point Objective (RPO) and Recovery Time Objective (RTO). These metrics define how much data loss and downtime are acceptable.

- **Critical Workloads:** Identify which workloads are mission-critical and require immediate recovery in case of a disaster.

- **Data Dependencies:** Understand data dependencies between different services and applications.

2. Choose the Right GCP Region

GCP OFFERS MULTIPLE regions and availability zones worldwide. When designing your DR plan, select a secondary GCP region that is geographically distant from your primary region. This ensures data redundancy and minimizes the risk of both regions being affected by the same disaster.

3. Replication Strategies

GCP PROVIDES VARIOUS replication strategies to ensure data redundancy:

- **Cloud Storage:** Use Cloud Storage's multi-region or dual-region buckets for storing critical data. Enable versioning and object lifecycle policies to manage data retention.

- **Database Replication:** If you're using Cloud SQL, Cloud Spanner, or other GCP databases, implement cross-region replication for your databases to ensure data availability.

4. Compute and Application Failover

CONSIDER HOW YOUR APPLICATIONS will failover to the secondary region. Options include:

- **Traffic Routing:** Use Google Cloud DNS or external global load balancers to route traffic to the secondary region in case of a primary region failure.

- **Compute Engine Instances:** Create replicas of your compute instances in the secondary region, ready to take over during a disaster. Use instance templates and managed instance groups for scalability.

5. Data Backup and Snapshot Policies

IMPLEMENT AUTOMATED backup and snapshot policies for your data and virtual machines. This ensures that you can restore to a known good state if necessary. Use Google Cloud Scheduler and Cloud Functions for automation.

6. Disaster Recovery Runbooks

CREATE DETAILED RUNBOOKS that document the steps to follow during a disaster recovery scenario. Include contact information, procedures, and a checklist for recovering critical services.

7. Regular Testing and Drills

REGULARLY TEST YOUR DR plan to ensure it works as expected. Conduct both planned and surprise drills to validate your team's readiness to respond to disasters.

8. Compliance and Security

ENSURE THAT YOUR DR plan complies with industry regulations and standards. Implement security best practices, including encryption, identity and access management (IAM), and audit logging.

9. Cost Management

OPTIMIZE YOUR DR RESOURCES to minimize costs. Use GCP's pricing calculator to estimate expenses and choose cost-effective storage and compute options.

10. Managed DR Services

CONSIDER USING GCP'S managed DR services like Google Cloud VMware Engine, which offers automated failover and recovery for VMware workloads.

11. Documentation and Training

DOCUMENT YOUR DR PLAN thoroughly and provide training to your staff. Ensure that all team members understand their roles and responsibilities during a disaster recovery event.

Case Study: E-commerce Website

IMAGINE AN E-COMMERCE company that operates its website on GCP. They have a disaster recovery plan that includes:

- Continuous data replication to a secondary GCP region using Cloud Storage and database replication.
- Traffic routing using Google Cloud DNS.
- Regular automated backups and snapshots.
- Detailed runbooks and a schedule for DR drills.
- Compliance with data privacy regulations.
- Cost-optimized resources for their secondary region.

In the event of a disaster, they can quickly failover to their secondary region, ensuring minimal data loss and downtime.

In conclusion, designing a disaster recovery plan on GCP involves careful assessment, selection of the right region, replication strategies, and thorough testing. By following best practices and leveraging GCP's services, organizations can create robust and resilient DR plans that protect their data and ensure business continuity.

Section 15.3: Data Replication and Backup Strategies

DATA REPLICATION AND backup strategies are fundamental components of a comprehensive disaster recovery (DR) plan on Google Cloud Platform (GCP). These strategies ensure data durability, availability, and recoverability in the event of unexpected disasters or data loss. In this section, we will delve into data replication and backup best practices on GCP.

1. Data Replication

a. Cloud Storage Multi-Region and Dual-Region Buckets

GOOGLE CLOUD STORAGE offers multi-region and dual-region storage options for data replication. Multi-region buckets replicate data across multiple regions, ensuring high availability and durability. Dual-region buckets replicate data synchronously between two regions. Choose the option that aligns with your DR requirements and compliance needs.

```
# Create a multi-region bucket

gsutil mb -l multi-region LOCATION gs://BUCKET_NAME

# Create a dual-region bucket

gsutil mb -l dual-region LOCATION gs://BUCKET_NAME
```

b. Object Versioning

ENABLE OBJECT VERSIONING in Cloud Storage to protect against accidental data deletion or modification. Object versioning allows you to retain and recover previous versions of objects.

```
# Enable versioning for a bucket

gsutil versioning set on gs://BUCKET_NAME
```

c. Database Replication

IF YOU'RE USING GCP databases like Cloud SQL or Cloud Spanner, implement cross-region replication for your databases. This ensures data availability and minimizes the risk of data loss.

2. Data Backup Strategies

a. Automated Backups

AUTOMATE DATA BACKUPS by scheduling regular snapshots of your critical data. Use Google Cloud Scheduler and Cloud Functions to create backup jobs.

```
# Example Cloud Scheduler job to trigger a backup

gcloud scheduler jobs create pubsub BACKUP_JOB_NAME \

—schedule="0 0 * * *" \

—topic=projects/PROJECT_ID/topics/BACKUP_TOPIC
```

b. Persistent Disk Snapshots

FOR VIRTUAL MACHINE (VM) instances using Persistent Disks, take snapshots to capture the VM's disk state at specific points in time. Schedule snapshot jobs to ensure data consistency.

 # Create a snapshot of a disk

gcloud compute disks snapshot INSTANCE_NAME—snapshot-names=SNAPSHOT_NAME

c. Data Lifecycle Policies

IMPLEMENT DATA LIFECYCLE policies in Cloud Storage to automate the management of object versions and retention periods. Configure rules to transition data to archival storage classes or delete it when it's no longer needed.

 # Create a lifecycle rule for a bucket

gsutil lifecycle set LIFECYCLE_RULE_FILE gs://BUCKET_NAME

3. Cross-Region Replication for Disaster Recovery

CROSS-REGION REPLICATION ensures that your data is stored in a geographically distant location, reducing the risk of data loss due to regional disasters. To set up cross-region replication:

a. Cloud Storage Cross-Region Replication

CONFIGURE CROSS-REGION replication for Cloud Storage buckets to replicate objects to a secondary region.

 # Enable cross-region replication for a bucket

gsutil versioning set on gs://BUCKET_NAME

gsutil iam ch serviceAccount:DESTINATION_SERVICE_ACCOUNT:objectCreato \

gs://BUCKET_NAME

b. Cross-Region Database Replication

FOR DATABASES LIKE Cloud SQL, set up cross-region replication to ensure database availability in a secondary region.

 # Example: Creating a read replica in a different region

gcloud sql instances create READER_INSTANCE_NAME—master-instance=MASTER_INSTAN \

—region=SECONDARY_REGION

4. Monitoring and Auditing

IMPLEMENT MONITORING and auditing solutions to track data replication status, backup job execution, and data access. Use Cloud Monitoring and Cloud Audit Logs to gain visibility into your data protection measures.

In summary, data replication and backup strategies are pivotal for ensuring data resilience and recoverability in a disaster recovery scenario on GCP. Leveraging GCP's storage options, automated backups, and cross-region replication capabilities, organizations can create robust data protection mechanisms that align with their DR requirements and compliance standards. Regular testing and monitoring further enhance the effectiveness of these strategies, ensuring data is safeguarded and recoverable when needed.

Section 15.4: Business Continuity Planning with GCP

BUSINESS CONTINUITY planning (BCP) is a critical aspect of disaster recovery (DR) preparedness on Google Cloud Platform (GCP). While disaster recovery focuses on data recovery and system restoration, BCP encompasses a broader perspective. It aims to ensure the continuity of essential business operations during and after a disruptive event. In this section, we will explore the key components of effective business continuity planning with GCP.

1. Business Impact Analysis (BIA)

BEFORE DEVELOPING A BCP, conduct a comprehensive business impact analysis. Identify critical business functions, dependencies, and recovery time objectives (RTOs). Understanding the impact of downtime on your organization is essential for prioritizing resources and efforts.

2. Redundancy and High Availability

UTILIZE GCP'S INFRASTRUCTURE capabilities to build redundancy and high availability into your architecture. Leverage services like Google Load Balancers, multi-region deployments, and autoscaling to ensure minimal downtime.

```
# Create an instance template with autoscaling

gcloud compute instance-templates create TEMPLATE_NAME \

—region=REGION \
```

—machine-type=MACHINE_TYPE \

—autoscaling-policy=POLICY_NAME

3. Data Backup and Replication

AS DISCUSSED IN PREVIOUS sections, implement robust data backup and replication strategies. Ensure that critical data is regularly backed up, and redundant copies are stored in different geographic locations.

4. Disaster Recovery as a Service (DRaaS)

CONSIDER USING DRAAS solutions available on GCP, such as Google Cloud VMware Engine. These services simplify DR planning by providing a seamless failover environment for virtualized workloads.

5. Cloud Endpoints for API Redundancy

IF YOUR BUSINESS RELIES on APIs, leverage Cloud Endpoints to create redundant API endpoints across multiple regions. This ensures API availability even if one region experiences disruptions.

 # Deploy an API with Cloud Endpoints

gcloud endpoints services deploy openapi.yaml

6. Communication and Collaboration Tools

ENSURE THAT YOUR ORGANIZATION has effective communication and collaboration tools in place. Google Workspace provides features like Gmail, Google Drive, and Google Meet, which can be instrumental in maintaining communication during disruptions.

7. Employee Training and Awareness

TRAIN EMPLOYEES ON BCP procedures and create awareness about their roles during a disruptive event. Conduct regular drills and tests to ensure everyone knows how to respond.

8. Incident Response Plan

DEVELOP AN INCIDENT response plan that outlines the steps to be taken in the event of a disruption. Define roles and responsibilities, and establish a chain of command for decision-making.

 # Sample incident response plan template

- Incident identification and classification

- Activation of the incident response team

- Containment and mitigation actions

- Communication and coordination

- Recovery and restoration efforts

- Post-incident evaluation and improvement

9. Compliance and Governance

ENSURE THAT YOUR BCP aligns with regulatory requirements and industry standards. Implement proper governance controls and compliance monitoring to avoid legal and financial repercussions.

10. Regular Testing and Updates

REGULARLY TEST YOUR BCP to validate its effectiveness. Conduct tabletop exercises, simulations, and actual failover tests to identify weaknesses and make necessary improvements.

11. Documentation and Documentation Management

MAINTAIN DETAILED DOCUMENTATION of your BCP, including procedures, contact lists, and recovery plans. Use tools like Google Docs and Google Drive to store and manage this documentation securely.

12. Partnering with Google Cloud Professional Services

CONSIDER ENGAGING WITH Google Cloud Professional Services or certified partners to design, implement, and optimize your BCP. They can provide expert guidance and support tailored to your organization's needs.

In conclusion, business continuity planning with GCP involves a holistic approach to ensure that critical business operations can continue during and after disruptions. By conducting a thorough business impact analysis, implementing redundancy, utilizing DRaaS, and focusing on communication and training, organizations can strengthen their resilience and minimize the impact of disruptive events. Regular testing, compliance adherence, and expert guidance further enhance the effectiveness of your BCP.

Section 15.5: Testing and Improving Your Disaster Recovery Plan

TESTING AND CONTINUOUS improvement are crucial aspects of any disaster recovery (DR) plan on Google Cloud Platform (GCP). Without regular testing, you can't be sure that your DR plan will work when it's needed most. In this section, we'll explore the importance of testing your DR plan and strategies for ongoing improvement.

1. Types of DR Testing

THERE ARE SEVERAL TYPES of DR testing methods to consider:

- **Full-Scale Testing**: This involves a complete failover to your DR environment to ensure everything works as expected. It's the most comprehensive but also the most disruptive type of test.

- **Partial Failover Testing**: In this approach, only a portion of your systems or applications is failed over to the DR environment. It's less disruptive than a full-scale test and allows you to test specific components.

- **Tabletop Exercises**: These are simulation-based tests where team members discuss and walk through DR scenarios without actually executing failover procedures. They are excellent for testing decision-making and communication.

- **Regular DR Drills**: Conduct scheduled drills to simulate real-world scenarios. These can include unplanned incidents and scheduled tests to validate RTOs and RPOs.

2. Automate Testing Procedures

AUTOMATION CAN STREAMLINE the testing process. Create scripts or use automation tools to execute failover and failback procedures. Automating tests ensures consistency and reduces the risk of human error.

 # Example script for automating VM failover

gcloud compute instances stop INSTANCE_NAME—zone=ZONE

3. Test Frequency

REGULARLY SCHEDULE and conduct DR tests. The frequency depends on your organization's needs, but quarterly or semi-annual tests are common. Frequent testing allows you to catch issues early and make improvements.

4. Test Documentation

DOCUMENT THE RESULTS of each test, including any issues or areas that need improvement. Use these findings to refine your DR plan. Consider creating an After-Action Report (AAR) to capture lessons learned.

5. Integration with Monitoring and Alerting

INTEGRATE YOUR DR TESTING with your monitoring and alerting systems. This ensures that you're aware of any issues during the testing process and can take corrective actions promptly.

 # Set up monitoring alerts for DR testing

```
gcloud monitoring policies create POLICY_NAME \
—display-name="DR Testing Alerts" \
—conditions=CONDITION1,CONDITION2
```

6. Involve Stakeholders

INCLUDE RELEVANT STAKEHOLDERS in the testing process. This may include IT teams, business units, and external partners. Ensuring that everyone is familiar with the DR plan and their roles is essential.

7. Scenario-Based Testing

CONDUCT TESTS BASED on different disaster scenarios. Test for scenarios like data center failures, network outages, and cyberattacks. Each scenario may require different procedures and responses.

8. Continuous Improvement

USE THE RESULTS OF your tests to continually improve your DR plan. Identify weaknesses, address them, and update your plan accordingly. Consider conducting "what-if" analyses to explore potential vulnerabilities.

9. Compliance and Audit

IF YOUR ORGANIZATION is subject to regulatory requirements, ensure that your DR tests align with compliance standards. Document the testing process to demonstrate compliance to auditors.

10. Review and Training

AFTER EACH TEST, HOLD a debriefing session to review the test's outcomes and discuss areas for improvement. Use these sessions as opportunities for additional training and awareness.

In conclusion, regular testing and improvement of your disaster recovery plan are essential to ensure its effectiveness. By testing different scenarios, automating procedures, involving stakeholders, and integrating testing with monitoring and alerting, you can maintain a robust DR strategy. Continuous improvement and documentation are key to staying prepared for unexpected disruptions and minimizing downtime.

Chapter 16: Cloud Automation and Infrastructure as Code

Chapter 16: Cloud Automation and Infrastructure as Code

Section 16.1: Automation in Cloud Computing

AUTOMATION IS A FUNDAMENTAL concept in cloud computing, enabling organizations to streamline operations, reduce manual intervention, and achieve greater efficiency. In this section, we'll explore the importance of automation in the cloud and how it can benefit businesses across various industries.

The Need for Automation

CLOUD ENVIRONMENTS are dynamic and highly scalable, which makes them powerful but also complex to manage. Manual provisioning and management of resources in the cloud can lead to errors, security vulnerabilities, and inefficiencies. Automation addresses these challenges by enabling the creation, configuration, and management of cloud resources through code.

Key Benefits of Automation

1. **Speed and Efficiency**: Automation allows for rapid resource provisioning and scaling, reducing the time required to deploy and manage infrastructure.
2. **Consistency**: Automation ensures that infrastructure is provisioned and configured consistently, eliminating configuration drift and reducing the risk of errors.
3. **Scalability**: Automated processes can scale resources up or down based on demand, ensuring optimal resource utilization and cost efficiency.

4. **Repeatability**: Infrastructure as Code (IaC) enables the replication of environments across different stages of development and testing, leading to more reliable deployments.
5. **Cost Control**: Automation can help optimize cloud costs by automatically scaling down or terminating resources when they are not in use.
6. **Security**: Automated security policies and configurations can be consistently applied to resources, reducing the risk of security vulnerabilities.

Infrastructure as Code (IaC)

INFRASTRUCTURE AS CODE (IaC) is a fundamental approach to automation in the cloud. It involves defining and managing infrastructure using code, which can be version-controlled, tested, and deployed programmatically. Popular IaC tools like Terraform and Google Cloud Deployment Manager provide a way to define cloud resources in code.

Use Cases for Automation

AUTOMATION IN THE CLOUD is applicable to various use cases, including:

• **Application Deployment**: Automating the deployment of applications, including the provisioning of servers, databases, and networking components.

• **Continuous Integration/Continuous Deployment (CI/CD)**: Implementing automated pipelines for building, testing, and deploying software applications.

- **Resource Scaling**: Automatically scaling resources based on traffic patterns, ensuring optimal performance and cost-efficiency.

- **Backup and Disaster Recovery**: Automating data backups and recovery processes to minimize downtime and data loss.

- **Security and Compliance**: Implementing automated security policies and compliance checks to enforce best practices.

- **Cost Optimization**: Implementing cost optimization strategies such as resource scheduling and auto-scaling.

Challenges of Automation

WHILE AUTOMATION OFFERS numerous advantages, it also presents challenges. These challenges include:

- **Learning Curve**: Teams need to learn and adapt to automation tools and practices.

- **Complexity**: Managing automation for large-scale environments can be complex.

- **Cost**: There may be initial costs associated with implementing automation.

- **Risk**: Misconfigurations in automated processes can lead to unintended consequences.

In the subsequent sections of this chapter, we will delve deeper into the principles and tools of Infrastructure as Code (IaC) and how to leverage automation effectively in Google Cloud Platform (GCP).

Section 16.2: Infrastructure as Code: Principles and Tools

IN THIS SECTION, WE'LL dive deeper into Infrastructure as Code (IaC), a fundamental approach to automating cloud infrastructure management. IaC enables you to define, provision, and manage cloud resources using code, bringing consistency, repeatability, and version control to your infrastructure. Let's explore the principles and tools associated with IaC.

Principles of Infrastructure as Code

1. Declarative vs. Imperative: IaC can be declarative or imperative. Declarative IaC defines what the desired end-state should be, allowing the automation tool to determine how to achieve it. Imperative IaC specifies both the desired state and the steps to reach it. Declarative IaC is generally preferred for its simplicity and safety.

2. Idempotence: IaC scripts should be idempotent, meaning they can be run multiple times without causing issues. Repeatedly applying the same IaC script should not result in unintended changes.

3. Version Control: Just like software code, IaC should be stored in a version control system (e.g., Git) to track changes, collaborate with team members, and roll back to previous configurations if needed.

4. Testing: IaC code should be subject to testing, including unit tests and integration tests, to catch errors and ensure that

configurations work as expected.

5. Documentation: Maintain clear and up-to-date documentation for your IaC code, describing the purpose of resources and their configurations.

IaC Tools and Technologies

THERE ARE SEVERAL TOOLS and technologies available for implementing IaC. Some popular choices include:

1. Terraform: Terraform is an open-source IaC tool by HashiCorp. It uses a declarative configuration language to define infrastructure resources and supports multiple cloud providers, including Google Cloud Platform (GCP).

2. Google Cloud Deployment Manager: GCP offers its own IaC solution called Deployment Manager. It allows you to define infrastructure using YAML or Jinja2 templates and is tightly integrated with GCP services.

3. Ansible: While Ansible is primarily known as a configuration management tool, it also offers IaC capabilities. It uses YAML-based playbooks to define infrastructure and can manage both on-premises and cloud resources.

4. Pulumi: Pulumi is an IaC tool that allows you to define infrastructure using familiar programming languages like Python, JavaScript, and TypeScript. It supports multiple cloud providers, including GCP.

5. Chef and Puppet: These configuration management tools can be used for IaC by defining resource configurations in code and managing infrastructure.

IaC Workflow

IMPLEMENTING IAC TYPICALLY follows a workflow:

1. **Define Infrastructure**: Write code that defines the desired infrastructure, specifying resources, configurations, and dependencies.
2. **Version Control**: Store the IaC code in a version control system (e.g., Git) to track changes and collaborate with team members.
3. **Testing**: Run tests to validate the IaC code, ensuring that it provisions resources correctly and meets requirements.
4. **Provision Resources**: Use the IaC tool to apply the code and provision the infrastructure. The tool will create, update, or delete resources as needed.
5. **Monitoring and Compliance**: Implement monitoring and compliance checks to ensure that the infrastructure remains in the desired state.
6. **Continuous Integration/Continuous Deployment (CI/CD)**: Integrate IaC into your CI/CD pipeline for automated deployments and updates.

Benefits of Infrastructure as Code

IMPLEMENTING IAC OFFERS several advantages:

- **Consistency**: IaC ensures that infrastructure is consistent across environments, reducing configuration drift.

- **Scalability**: IaC simplifies resource scaling by allowing you to define and replicate configurations easily.

- **Versioning**: IaC code can be versioned, making it easier to track changes and roll back if necessary.
- **Collaboration**: Teams can collaborate effectively by using version control and standardized IaC practices.
- **Efficiency**: Automating infrastructure tasks reduces manual effort and speeds up deployments.

In the subsequent sections of this chapter, we will explore practical examples of using IaC tools like Terraform and Google Cloud Deployment Manager to automate infrastructure provisioning on Google Cloud Platform.

Section 16.3: Using Deployment Manager and Terraform on GCP

IN THIS SECTION, WE will delve into the practical aspects of using Google Cloud Platform's Deployment Manager and Terraform for Infrastructure as Code (IaC). These tools empower you to define and automate your infrastructure provisioning on GCP.

Deployment Manager on Google Cloud Platform

GOOGLE CLOUD DEPLOYMENT Manager is a native IaC tool designed to work seamlessly with GCP services. It allows you to define your infrastructure using YAML or Jinja2 templates and then deploy and manage that infrastructure as a deployment. Here's how you can use Deployment Manager:

1. **Define Your Configuration**: Start by creating a YAML or Jinja2 template that describes the resources you want to create, such as virtual machines, networks, and databases. You can also specify the properties of these resources, like

their names, sizes, and regions.

2. **Deployment Creation**: Use the gcloud command-line tool or the GCP Console to create a deployment. You'll provide the path to your configuration file and any necessary parameters.
3. **Deployment Updates**: If you need to make changes to your infrastructure, simply update the configuration file and apply the changes. Deployment Manager will determine the necessary actions to bring your infrastructure in line with the new configuration.
4. **Version Control**: Store your Deployment Manager configuration files in a version control system like Git to track changes and collaborate with others.
5. **Monitoring and Management**: GCP provides monitoring and management capabilities for your deployments, allowing you to view the state of your infrastructure and make adjustments as needed.

Terraform on Google Cloud Platform

TERRAFORM IS AN OPEN-source IaC tool developed by HashiCorp. It's known for its flexibility and support for multi-cloud environments, including GCP. Here's how you can use Terraform on GCP:

1. **Install Terraform**: Start by installing Terraform on your local machine. Terraform provides a command-line interface for managing your infrastructure.
2. **Define Your Configuration**: Create a Terraform configuration file (usually with a .tf extension) that defines the resources and their properties. You'll use HashiCorp Configuration Language (HCL) to express your infrastructure.

3. **Initialize the Project**: Use the terraform init command to initialize your project. This will download the necessary providers (in this case, the GCP provider) and set up your working directory.
4. **Plan and Apply**: Run terraform plan to see the changes that Terraform will make to your infrastructure based on your configuration. To apply these changes, use terraform apply.
5. **Version Control**: Just like with Deployment Manager, store your Terraform configuration files in a version control system to manage changes and collaborate with teammates.
6. **State Management**: Terraform keeps track of your infrastructure's state, which is essential for making changes without recreating resources. You can store the state locally or in remote backends like Google Cloud Storage.
7. **Monitoring and Management**: GCP provides monitoring and management tools that you can use in conjunction with Terraform to monitor your resources and their health.

Choosing Between Deployment Manager and Terraform

THE CHOICE BETWEEN Google Cloud Deployment Manager and Terraform often depends on your team's familiarity with the tools and your specific requirements. Some factors to consider:

- **Native vs. Multi-Cloud**: Deployment Manager is native to GCP, making it tightly integrated with GCP services. Terraform, on the other hand, supports multiple cloud providers and on-premises infrastructure, which can be beneficial for multi-cloud strategies.

- **Complexity and Flexibility**: Terraform is known for its flexibility and can be used to manage resources outside of GCP. If you require intricate control over your infrastructure or work with multiple cloud providers, Terraform might be a better fit.

- **Team Skillset**: Consider your team's existing skills and experience with IaC tools. Training and familiarity with a specific tool may influence your choice.

In practice, some organizations use both tools, leveraging Deployment Manager for GCP-specific resources and Terraform for multi-cloud or more complex deployments.

In the next sections, we'll provide hands-on examples of using both Deployment Manager and Terraform to provision resources on Google Cloud Platform.

Section 16.4: Automating Deployments and Maintenance

AUTOMATION IS A FUNDAMENTAL aspect of managing cloud infrastructure efficiently. In this section, we'll explore various aspects of automating deployments and ongoing maintenance tasks in Google Cloud Platform (GCP). This includes strategies for continuous integration and continuous deployment (CI/CD), as well as automating routine tasks using Google Cloud's automation tools.

Continuous Integration and Continuous Deployment (CI/CD)

CI/CD IS A SOFTWARE development practice that focuses on automating the building, testing, and deployment of applications.

It ensures that code changes are automatically built, tested, and deployed to production, reducing the risk of errors and streamlining the development process.

In GCP, you can achieve CI/CD using services like Cloud Build and Cloud Source Repositories:

1. **Cloud Build**: Google Cloud Build is a fully managed CI/CD platform that automates build, test, and deployment pipelines. It integrates with various source code repositories, including Google Cloud Source Repositories, GitHub, and Bitbucket.
2. **Cloud Source Repositories**: Google Cloud Source Repositories is a Git repository hosting service that allows you to store and manage your source code. It seamlessly integrates with Cloud Build, enabling you to set up CI/CD pipelines.

With these tools, you can define automated pipelines that trigger on code changes, automatically build and test your applications, and then deploy them to the appropriate environments. This helps maintain code quality and ensures that new features and bug fixes can be quickly delivered to users.

Automation Tools in Google Cloud

GOOGLE CLOUD OFFERS several automation tools and services to simplify routine tasks and manage resources efficiently:

1. **Cloud Scheduler**: Google Cloud Scheduler is a fully managed cron job service that allows you to automate the execution of tasks at specified intervals. It integrates with various GCP services, making it easy to automate tasks like data backups or resource scaling.

2. **Cloud Functions**: Cloud Functions is a serverless compute service that lets you run event-driven code without managing infrastructure. You can trigger functions in response to events from other GCP services or external sources.
3. **Cloud Composer**: Google Cloud Composer is a managed Apache Airflow service that allows you to automate, schedule, and monitor workflows. It's particularly useful for complex data processing and ETL tasks.
4. **Cloud Monitoring and Logging**: Google Cloud's monitoring and logging tools provide insights into the health and performance of your infrastructure. You can set up alerts to automate responses to specific events or issues.
5. **Identity and Access Management (IAM)**: Automate access control and permissions management using IAM policies. Create custom roles and use policy hierarchies to enforce security best practices.
6. **Cloud Deployment Manager and Terraform**: As discussed in previous sections, these tools enable you to automate the provisioning and management of your infrastructure as code.

Infrastructure as Code (IaC) Best Practices

TO EFFECTIVELY AUTOMATE deployments and maintenance, consider the following best practices:

- **Version Control**: Store your infrastructure code in version control systems like Git. This ensures that changes are tracked, and you can collaborate with team members.

- **Modularization**: Organize your IaC code into reusable modules or templates. This simplifies management and allows you to apply consistent configurations across different environments.

- **Testing**: Implement automated testing for your infrastructure code. Test your templates and configurations to catch errors before deployment.

- **Documentation**: Maintain clear and up-to-date documentation for your infrastructure. This helps team members understand the setup and configuration.

- **Security**: Apply security best practices when writing your automation code. This includes safeguarding credentials and minimizing exposure of sensitive information.

Automation is a critical component of managing cloud resources efficiently and consistently. By embracing CI/CD practices and leveraging GCP's automation tools, you can streamline your workflows, reduce manual intervention, and improve the reliability of your cloud infrastructure. In the next section, we'll explore best practices for cloud automation.

Section 16.5: Best Practices for Cloud Automation

IN THIS FINAL SECTION of Chapter 16, we'll delve into best practices for cloud automation in Google Cloud Platform (GCP). Effective automation not only streamlines operations but also ensures the security, reliability, and efficiency of your cloud infrastructure.

1. Define Clear Objectives: Before implementing

automation, clearly define your objectives and what you want to achieve. Determine the key tasks or processes that would benefit from automation.

2. Start Small: If you're new to automation, start with small, well-defined tasks. As you gain experience and confidence, gradually expand automation to more complex processes.

3. Use Infrastructure as Code (IaC): Implement IaC principles using tools like Google Deployment Manager or Terraform. This allows you to version control your infrastructure, manage it as code, and easily replicate environments.

4. Apply the Principle of Least Privilege: When configuring automation scripts and tools, follow the principle of least privilege (POLP). Ensure that automation processes only have the necessary permissions to perform their tasks, reducing security risks.

5. Regularly Review and Update: Automation scripts and configurations should be regularly reviewed and updated. As your infrastructure evolves, your automation should adapt accordingly.

6. Documentation and Comments: Document your automation scripts and configurations thoroughly. Include comments to explain complex or critical sections. This helps other team members understand and troubleshoot.

7. Testing and Validation: Implement automated testing for your automation code. Test deployments,

configurations, and workflows to catch errors before they affect production environments.

8. Backup and Recovery: Consider automated backup and recovery processes. Regularly back up critical data and configurations, and ensure that recovery processes are tested and reliable.

9. Monitor Automation: Use monitoring and alerting tools to keep an eye on your automation processes. Set up alerts for failures or unexpected behavior so that you can respond promptly.

10. Scalability and Performance: Design automation with scalability in mind. Ensure that your automation can handle increased workloads as your infrastructure grows.

11. Security Automation: Automate security checks and compliance audits. This includes scanning for vulnerabilities, ensuring proper access controls, and maintaining encryption standards.

12. Lifecycle Management: Implement automation for resource lifecycle management. Automatically decommission resources that are no longer needed to optimize costs.

13. Collaboration: Encourage collaboration among team members working on automation. Use version control systems and collaboration platforms to share and manage code.

14. Disaster Recovery Testing: Regularly test your disaster recovery processes and automation to ensure

they work as expected during critical situations.

15. Keep Abreast of Updates: Stay informed about updates and changes in the cloud environment, as they may impact your automation. Ensure that your scripts and configurations are up to date.

16. Training and Skill Development: Invest in training and skill development for your team members involved in automation. Staying current with best practices and new tools is essential.

17. Cost Optimization: Use automation to monitor and optimize costs. Implement policies that automatically scale resources based on demand or shut down idle resources.

18. Review and Audit Logs: Enable and regularly review logs generated by your automation processes. This helps in troubleshooting issues and maintaining transparency.

19. Compliance and Governance: Implement automation to enforce compliance policies and governance standards across your cloud environment.

20. Feedback Loop: Establish a feedback loop with your team and stakeholders. Continuously gather feedback to identify areas for improvement in your automation processes.

BY FOLLOWING THESE best practices, you can harness the full potential of cloud automation in GCP. Automation not only saves time and resources but also enhances the overall quality and reliability of your cloud infrastructure. As you embark on your automation journey, remember that it's an ongoing process of improvement and adaptation to changing requirements and technologies.

Chapter 17: Monitoring, Logging, and Diagnostics

Section 17.1: Essentials of Cloud Monitoring

IN TODAY'S CLOUD-CENTRIC world, monitoring, logging, and diagnostics are fundamental aspects of managing and maintaining a cloud infrastructure effectively. In this section, we will explore the essentials of cloud monitoring in Google Cloud Platform (GCP) and why it's crucial for operational success.

What is Cloud Monitoring?

CLOUD MONITORING REFERS to the practice of observing and collecting data from various resources in a cloud environment to assess their performance, health, and availability. This data is then used to identify issues, troubleshoot problems, and make informed decisions to optimize resource utilization and ensure a seamless user experience.

The Importance of Cloud Monitoring

1. **Proactive Issue Detection**: Cloud monitoring allows you to detect and address issues before they impact your users. By setting up alerts and thresholds, you can be notified of abnormal behavior or performance degradation in real-time.
2. **Performance Optimization**: Monitoring data provides insights into the performance of your cloud resources. You can identify bottlenecks, optimize configurations, and improve resource allocation based on these insights.
3. **Resource Utilization**: Understanding how your resources

are utilized helps in cost optimization. You can rightsize instances, identify idle resources, and implement auto-scaling to match demand.

4. **Availability and Reliability**: Monitoring ensures high availability and reliability. By tracking uptime and response times, you can meet service-level agreements (SLAs) and maintain a positive user experience.
5. **Security**: Monitoring is vital for security. You can detect unusual activities, unauthorized access, or security breaches by analyzing logs and monitoring user activities.

Key Components of Cloud Monitoring

1. **Metrics**: Metrics are quantitative data points that represent the behavior of resources or services. GCP provides a wide range of predefined metrics, and you can create custom metrics to suit your specific needs.
2. **Logs**: Logs are textual records of events and activities within your cloud environment. They provide detailed information about resource interactions, errors, and system events. GCP's Cloud Logging allows you to store, analyze, and retrieve logs efficiently.
3. **Alerting Policies**: Alerting policies define conditions and thresholds for triggering notifications. You can set up alerts to notify you via email, SMS, or other channels when specific conditions are met.
4. **Dashboards**: Dashboards are customizable views that display important metrics and data in a visually appealing format. They help you gain insights at a glance and can be shared with team members.
5. **Diagnostics Tools**: GCP offers various diagnostic tools, such as Cloud Trace and Cloud Debugger, to troubleshoot and debug applications and services effectively.

Monitoring Best Practices

TO MAKE THE MOST OF cloud monitoring in GCP, consider the following best practices:

- Define clear objectives and key performance indicators (KPIs) for your monitoring strategy.

- Regularly review and refine your alerting policies to avoid false positives and negatives.

- Use dashboards to visualize metrics and create custom views tailored to your needs.

- Implement centralized logging to consolidate logs from multiple sources for easier analysis.

- Leverage anomaly detection and machine learning capabilities for advanced monitoring.

- Continuously monitor costs associated with monitoring itself to avoid unexpected expenses.

In conclusion, cloud monitoring is an integral part of managing a cloud infrastructure effectively. It empowers you to proactively address issues, optimize performance, ensure reliability, and enhance security. By following best practices and leveraging the monitoring tools available in GCP, you can maintain a robust and resilient cloud environment.

Section 17.2: Deep Dive into Cloud Logging

IN THE PREVIOUS SECTION, we introduced the essentials of cloud monitoring. Now, let's take a deep dive into one of the crucial components of cloud monitoring in Google Cloud Platform (GCP) - Cloud Logging.

What is Cloud Logging?

CLOUD LOGGING, FORMERLY known as Stackdriver Logging, is a comprehensive log management solution provided by GCP. It allows you to store, search, analyze, and monitor log data generated by your cloud resources and applications. Logs provide valuable insights into the behavior of your systems, helping you troubleshoot issues, ensure security, and gain operational visibility.

Key Features of Cloud Logging:

1. **Centralized Log Storage**: Cloud Logging provides a centralized repository for logs from various GCP services and external sources. This centralization simplifies log management and analysis.
2. **Scalability**: Cloud Logging can handle a massive volume of logs, making it suitable for both small-scale and large-scale applications. You can store logs for extended periods without worrying about storage constraints.
3. **Powerful Querying**: The Query Builder in Cloud Logging allows you to create complex queries to filter and extract specific log entries. You can search logs based on various criteria, including time range, severity, and custom labels.
4. **Real-Time Analysis**: Cloud Logging provides real-time log ingestion and analysis, ensuring you have up-to-the-minute insights into your applications and infrastructure.
5. **Alerting and Notifications**: You can set up alerting policies based on log entries. When predefined conditions are met, Cloud Logging can trigger notifications through various channels like email, SMS, or PagerDuty.

6. **Integration with Other GCP Services**: Cloud Logging seamlessly integrates with other GCP services like Cloud Monitoring and Cloud Trace, allowing you to correlate logs with metrics and traces for in-depth analysis.
7. **Log Exports**: You can export logs to other Google Cloud services or external destinations like Google Cloud Storage, BigQuery, Pub/Sub, and more. This enables advanced analytics and long-term retention strategies.

Types of Logs in Cloud Logging:

CLOUD LOGGING COLLECTS various types of logs, including:

- **Audit Logs**: These logs record activities related to the management of GCP resources, such as who performed an action, when, and what the action was.

- **System Logs**: System logs contain information about the behavior and performance of GCP resources, including virtual machines, containers, and network components.

- **Application Logs**: Application logs are generated by your applications and services. They provide insights into application-specific events and errors.

Log Severity Levels:

LOG ENTRIES IN CLOUD Logging are categorized into severity levels, which help you prioritize and filter logs based on their importance:

- **DEBUG**: Information useful for debugging and troubleshooting.
- **INFO**: General informational messages.
- **NOTICE**: Normal but significant events.
- **WARNING**: Events that may indicate a problem.
- **ERROR**: Events that indicate a significant problem.
- **CRITICAL**: Critical events that require immediate attention.
- **ALERT**: Events that should be addressed urgently.
- **EMERGENCY**: Emergency events requiring immediate action.

Using Cloud Logging

TO START USING CLOUD Logging, you need to:

1. Enable Cloud Logging for your project.
2. Configure the log sources, specifying which logs to collect.
3. Write log entries from your applications using the appropriate client libraries or APIs.
4. Create log-based metrics and alerting policies as needed.

For example, you can use the google-cloud-logging library for Python to interact with Cloud Logging programmatically:

```
from google.cloud import logging

# Create a client

client = logging.Client()
```

```
# Write a log entry

logger = client.logger("my-log")

logger.log_text("This is an example log entry.", severity="INFO")
```

With Cloud Logging, you can gain deep insights into your applications and infrastructure, helping you troubleshoot issues, monitor performance, and enhance security effectively. It plays a critical role in maintaining the reliability and stability of your cloud-based systems.

Section 17.3: Implementing Effective Diagnostic Strategies

IN THE REALM OF CLOUD computing, monitoring and diagnostics are indispensable components of maintaining a healthy and efficient system. While Section 17.1 introduced the essentials of cloud monitoring, and Section 17.2 delved into Cloud Logging, this section explores strategies and best practices for implementing effective diagnostic strategies in Google Cloud Platform (GCP).

The Importance of Diagnostics

DIAGNOSTICS ARE THE means by which you identify, analyze, and resolve issues within your cloud environment. They play a vital role in ensuring system reliability, performance optimization, and timely troubleshooting. Effective diagnostics help in identifying the root causes of problems, which is essential for maintaining the availability of your applications and services.

Diagnostic Strategies in GCP

1. **Use Monitoring Metrics**: GCP provides a wealth of

metrics that offer insights into various aspects of your resources and applications. Utilize these metrics to gain an understanding of resource utilization, system behavior, and performance trends. Create custom dashboards to visualize these metrics in real-time.

2. **Alerting and Notifications**: Set up proactive alerting based on predefined thresholds and conditions. Leverage Cloud Monitoring to create alerting policies that notify you when specific events or metrics reach critical levels. Notifications can be sent via email, SMS, or integration with third-party incident management tools like PagerDuty.
3. **Custom Logs**: Beyond standard logs, consider creating custom logs that capture application-specific events and errors. These logs provide tailored insights into your application's behavior, which can be invaluable for debugging and troubleshooting.
4. **Trace Analysis**: Use distributed tracing tools like Cloud Trace to gain visibility into the latency and performance of your application's components. Distributed tracing helps identify bottlenecks and areas for optimization in microservices architectures.
5. **Anomaly Detection**: Implement anomaly detection mechanisms to automatically identify abnormal behavior within your system. Machine learning-based anomaly detection can help in early detection of issues, reducing manual effort and response time.
6. **Error Reporting**: Take advantage of Error Reporting in GCP, which automatically captures and reports application errors. Error Reporting aggregates errors, provides context, and offers insights into the frequency and impact of errors.

7. **Debugging Tools**: Utilize debugging tools like Cloud Debugger, which allows you to inspect and debug applications running in production without disrupting the live environment. This is particularly useful for diagnosing complex issues.
8. **Incident Response Playbooks**: Develop incident response playbooks that outline the steps to be taken when issues arise. These playbooks should include roles and responsibilities, communication plans, and predefined actions for different scenarios.
9. **Data Analysis**: Use BigQuery and Data Studio to perform in-depth analysis of logs, metrics, and traces. These tools enable you to identify patterns, trends, and correlations that might not be apparent through standard monitoring.
10. **Continuous Improvement**: Regularly review and refine your diagnostic strategies. As your applications evolve, so should your diagnostic approaches. Ensure that lessons learned from incidents are used to enhance your monitoring and diagnostic capabilities.

Implementing Diagnostic Strategies

IMPLEMENTING EFFECTIVE diagnostic strategies in GCP involves a combination of configuring monitoring and logging, setting up alerting policies, and continuously analyzing data. It's an ongoing process that requires collaboration between development, operations, and site reliability engineering (SRE) teams to ensure a robust and responsive approach to maintaining system health.

By embracing diagnostic strategies in your cloud environment, you can proactively address issues, optimize performance, and enhance the overall reliability and availability of your applications and services hosted on Google Cloud Platform.

Section 17.4: Using Cloud Debugger and Cloud Trace

IN THIS SECTION, WE explore two essential tools provided by Google Cloud Platform (GCP) for advanced diagnostics and debugging: **Cloud Debugger** and **Cloud Trace**. These tools enable developers and operators to gain deeper insights into the behavior and performance of applications running on GCP.

Cloud Debugger

CLOUD DEBUGGER is a powerful debugging tool that allows you to inspect and debug applications in real-time, even in a production environment, without affecting your live application. It helps you identify and fix issues without the need for code redeployment or restarting the application.

Key features of Cloud Debugger include:

1. **Breakpoints**: You can set breakpoints in your code, just like in a traditional debugger. When a breakpoint is hit, Cloud Debugger captures a snapshot of the application's state, including variable values and call stacks.
2. **Stackdriver Integration**: Cloud Debugger is integrated with Google's Stackdriver, which means you can view captured snapshots and logs within the Stackdriver Debugger interface.
3. **Language Support**: Cloud Debugger supports multiple programming languages, including Java, Python, Node.js, Go, and Ruby, making it versatile for various application stacks.
4. **Zero-Impact Debugging**: Debugging with Cloud Debugger doesn't require code changes, recompilation, or application restarts. This ensures minimal disruption to

your application's operation.

5. **Production Debugging**: Cloud Debugger is designed for debugging in production. It allows you to debug live applications without affecting their availability or performance.
6. **Security**: Debugging sessions are secure and authenticated. Only authorized users can access and use Cloud Debugger to ensure data privacy and application security.

Cloud Trace

CLOUD TRACE is a distributed tracing tool that helps you understand and optimize the performance of your applications. It provides insights into how requests flow through various components of your application, highlighting latency bottlenecks and performance issues.

Key features of Cloud Trace include:

1. **Request Tracing**: Cloud Trace traces the journey of requests as they move through your application, showing the duration of each operation.
2. **Latency Analysis**: You can identify areas of high latency in your application by analyzing trace data. This is crucial for optimizing performance.
3. **Integration with GCP Services**: Cloud Trace seamlessly integrates with other GCP services, such as App Engine, Google Kubernetes Engine (GKE), and Cloud Functions, making it easy to trace requests in those environments.
4. **Custom Traces**: You can add custom trace data to your application code to gain more specific insights into how different parts of your application are performing.
5. **Service-Level Objectives (SLOs)**: With Cloud Trace, you

can define SLOs for your application's latency, and it will help you monitor and alert on deviations from these objectives.

6. **Error Tracking**: Cloud Trace also tracks errors and exceptions within your application, providing context to help diagnose and resolve issues.

Using Cloud Debugger and Cloud Trace Together

COMBINING CLOUD DEBUGGER and Cloud Trace provides a powerful debugging and performance optimization toolkit. When an issue is identified through Cloud Trace, you can use Cloud Debugger to inspect the code, variables, and state of your application at specific points in time. This integrated approach streamlines the debugging process and accelerates issue resolution.

In conclusion, Cloud Debugger and Cloud Trace are essential tools for diagnosing and improving the performance of applications on Google Cloud Platform. They enable developers and operators to maintain the reliability and responsiveness of their applications while minimizing disruption and downtime.

Section 17.5: Proactive Monitoring and Alerting Systems

IN THIS FINAL SECTION of Chapter 17, we explore the importance of proactive monitoring and alerting systems in managing and maintaining applications and infrastructure in the cloud. Proactive monitoring is a critical aspect of ensuring the reliability, availability, and performance of your services. It allows you to identify and address issues before they impact your users or business operations.

The Need for Proactive Monitoring

IN THE DYNAMIC AND ever-changing landscape of cloud computing, traditional reactive monitoring is no longer sufficient. Waiting for an application or system to fail before taking action can result in downtime, loss of revenue, and damage to your organization's reputation. Proactive monitoring takes a more preventive approach by continuously checking the health and performance of your resources and services.

Key reasons for adopting proactive monitoring include:

1. **Early Issue Detection**: Proactive monitoring detects anomalies, performance degradation, and potential issues in real-time or near real-time. This early detection allows you to address problems before they escalate.
2. **Improved Service Reliability**: By identifying and resolving issues proactively, you can enhance the reliability and availability of your services, ensuring a better user experience.
3. **Cost Savings**: Addressing issues early can prevent costly downtime and outages. It also allows for more efficient resource allocation and cost management.
4. **Compliance and Security**: Proactive monitoring helps in ensuring compliance with security and privacy regulations by detecting and responding to security threats and vulnerabilities promptly.
5. **Business Continuity**: With proactive monitoring, you can ensure business continuity by minimizing disruptions and maintaining service levels even during unexpected events.

Components of Proactive Monitoring

PROACTIVE MONITORING systems typically consist of the following components:

1. **Data Collection**: Collecting data from various sources, including servers, applications, network devices, and cloud services. This data can include metrics, logs, and events.
2. **Alerting Rules**: Defining alerting rules and thresholds based on acceptable performance and health criteria. When these thresholds are breached, alerts are generated.
3. **Alerting and Notification**: Configuring alerting and notification mechanisms to inform relevant teams or individuals when an alert is triggered. This can include email notifications, SMS alerts, or integration with incident management tools.
4. **Dashboard and Visualization**: Creating dashboards and visualizations to provide real-time insights into the state of your infrastructure and applications. Visualization tools help in quickly identifying trends and anomalies.
5. **Incident Response**: Establishing incident response procedures and workflows to address alerts efficiently. This includes defining roles and responsibilities for incident resolution.
6. **Automation**: Automating responses to common issues and alerts. Automation can help in resolving known issues quickly without manual intervention.

Choosing the Right Proactive Monitoring Tools

SELECTING THE APPROPRIATE proactive monitoring tools and services is crucial. Google Cloud Platform offers several tools and services to support proactive monitoring and alerting, including

Stackdriver Monitoring, Stackdriver Logging, and Stackdriver Trace. These tools provide comprehensive capabilities for monitoring, logging, and tracing across GCP services and resources.

When choosing proactive monitoring tools, consider the following factors:

1. **Scalability**: Ensure that the chosen tools can scale with your growing infrastructure and application needs.
2. **Integration**: Look for tools that seamlessly integrate with your existing infrastructure, applications, and cloud services.
3. **Customization**: The ability to define custom alerting rules and thresholds is essential to tailor monitoring to your specific requirements.
4. **Ease of Use**: User-friendly interfaces and dashboards simplify the setup and management of monitoring solutions.
5. **Cost-Efficiency**: Evaluate the cost implications of the chosen tools, including any pricing models or charges associated with monitoring.
6. **Community and Support**: Consider the availability of a supportive community and professional support options for troubleshooting and guidance.

In conclusion, proactive monitoring and alerting systems are fundamental for maintaining the health, performance, and reliability of cloud-based applications and infrastructure. They empower organizations to detect, respond to, and mitigate issues promptly, ensuring a seamless user experience and business continuity in the cloud environment. Choosing the right proactive monitoring tools and establishing effective monitoring practices is a key part of any cloud management strategy.

Chapter 18: Compliance, Governance, and Legal Considerations

Section 18.1: Navigating Compliance and Governance in the Cloud

IN THE EVER-EVOLVING landscape of cloud computing, compliance and governance play a crucial role in ensuring the security, privacy, and regulatory adherence of cloud-based solutions. This section explores the challenges and best practices for navigating compliance and governance requirements in the cloud.

The Importance of Compliance and Governance

COMPLIANCE REFERS TO the adherence to specific laws, regulations, standards, and industry-specific requirements that pertain to data privacy, security, and the overall operation of cloud services. Governance, on the other hand, involves the policies, processes, and controls that an organization puts in place to manage and oversee its cloud environment effectively.

Key reasons why compliance and governance are essential in the cloud include:

1. **Data Protection**: Compliance frameworks, such as GDPR, HIPAA, or PCI DSS, enforce data protection and privacy. Adhering to these frameworks is crucial for safeguarding sensitive information.
2. **Legal and Regulatory Requirements**: Many industries have specific regulatory requirements. Compliance ensures that organizations meet these requirements, avoiding legal consequences and fines.

3. **Risk Management**: Effective governance practices help identify and mitigate risks associated with cloud services, ensuring business continuity and resilience.
4. **Security**: Compliance often goes hand in hand with security. Meeting compliance standards enhances the security posture of cloud environments.
5. **Customer Trust**: Demonstrating compliance and strong governance builds trust with customers who are concerned about the safety of their data and the reliability of services.

Common Compliance Frameworks

NUMEROUS COMPLIANCE frameworks and standards apply to cloud environments. Some of the most prevalent ones include:

1. **General Data Protection Regulation (GDPR)**: GDPR regulates the protection of personal data for individuals within the European Union (EU). It imposes strict requirements on the handling of personal data, including data breach notification and user consent.
2. **Health Insurance Portability and Accountability Act (HIPAA)**: HIPAA sets standards for protecting sensitive patient data in the healthcare industry, ensuring confidentiality, integrity, and availability.
3. **Payment Card Industry Data Security Standard (PCI DSS)**: PCI DSS is designed to protect credit cardholder data. It applies to organizations that process, store, or transmit credit card information.
4. **National Institute of Standards and Technology (NIST) Framework**: NIST provides a comprehensive framework for enhancing cybersecurity. It is widely adopted for securing cloud environments.
5. **ISO/IEC 27001**: This international standard outlines best

practices for information security management systems (ISMS). It is a globally recognized framework for ensuring the confidentiality, integrity, and availability of data.

Best Practices for Cloud Compliance and Governance

ACHIEVING AND MAINTAINING compliance and governance in the cloud requires a strategic approach. Here are some best practices:

1. **Assessment and Planning**: Begin by assessing your organization's compliance needs and risks. Develop a comprehensive plan that outlines compliance goals, timelines, and responsibilities.
2. **Continuous Monitoring**: Implement continuous monitoring to track compliance status and detect any deviations promptly. Leverage cloud monitoring and security tools for this purpose.
3. **Data Encryption**: Encrypt data at rest and in transit. Encryption is a fundamental security measure to protect sensitive information.
4. **Access Controls**: Implement strict access controls and role-based access management (RBAC) to ensure that only authorized personnel can access critical resources.
5. **Audit Trails**: Maintain audit trails and logs to track system activities and access. Regularly review and analyze these logs for any suspicious activities.
6. **Vendor Assessment**: If using cloud service providers, assess their compliance certifications and security measures. Ensure that they align with your organization's requirements.
7. **Security Training**: Provide security and compliance

training to your staff to raise awareness and ensure everyone understands their role in compliance and governance.

8. **Incident Response**: Develop an incident response plan to address security breaches and compliance violations promptly.
9. **Regular Audits**: Conduct regular compliance audits and assessments to identify and rectify any non-compliance issues.
10. **Documentation**: Maintain detailed records of compliance efforts, policies, and procedures. Documentation is essential for demonstrating compliance to auditors or regulators.

Conclusion

NAVIGATING COMPLIANCE and governance in the cloud is a multifaceted task that requires a combination of technical measures, policies, and processes. Organizations must stay informed about evolving regulations, assess their specific compliance needs, and adopt best practices to ensure that their cloud-based operations remain secure, compliant, and resilient. By following these guidelines, businesses can leverage the cloud's benefits while adhering to legal and regulatory requirements.

Section 18.2: Understanding Legal and Regulatory Frameworks

IN THE CONTEXT OF CLOUD computing, understanding the legal and regulatory frameworks that govern data and technology is paramount. Various laws and regulations worldwide can impact how organizations use cloud services, handle data, and ensure compliance. This section delves into the key legal and regulatory considerations in the cloud.

International Data Laws and Privacy Regulations

1. General Data Protection Regulation (GDPR)

GDPR, ENFORCED IN THE European Union (EU), is one of the most stringent data protection regulations globally. It places strict controls on how personal data is collected, processed, and stored. Organizations handling EU citizens' data must comply with GDPR's requirements, including data subject rights, consent mechanisms, and mandatory data breach reporting.

2. California Consumer Privacy Act (CCPA)

CALIFORNIA'S CCPA GRANTS consumers more control over their personal information held by businesses. It mandates transparency about data collection, the right to request data deletion, and the right to opt-out of data selling. Organizations with customers in California must adhere to CCPA if certain revenue and data processing thresholds are met.

3. HIPAA and HITECH Act

IN THE UNITED STATES, the Health Insurance Portability and Accountability Act (HIPAA) and the Health Information Technology for Economic and Clinical Health (HITECH) Act regulate the healthcare industry's use of electronic health records. Cloud service providers handling protected health information (PHI) must sign HIPAA Business Associate Agreements (BAAs) to ensure compliance.

Data Sovereignty and Cross-Border Data Transfers

1. Data Sovereignty

DATA SOVEREIGNTY REFERS to the legal concept that data is subject to the laws and governance structures of the country where it is located. It means that data stored in a specific country must comply with that country's laws, even if the data owner is located elsewhere. Organizations must consider data sovereignty when choosing cloud regions for data storage.

2. EU-US Privacy Shield and Schrems II Decision

THE EU-US PRIVACY SHIELD was a framework for data transfers between the EU and the US. However, it was invalidated by the Schrems II decision in 2020. Now, organizations must rely on Standard Contractual Clauses (SCCs) or Binding Corporate Rules (BCRs) to transfer personal data from the EU to the US.

Cybersecurity and Incident Reporting

1. Cybersecurity Laws and Regulations

MANY COUNTRIES HAVE enacted cybersecurity laws and regulations to combat cyber threats. These laws may require organizations to implement specific security measures, report security incidents promptly, and protect sensitive data.

2. Mandatory Data Breach Notification

IN VARIOUS JURISDICTIONS, including the EU under GDPR, organizations are required to notify relevant authorities and affected individuals of data breaches promptly. Failure to do so can result in substantial fines.

Intellectual Property and Licensing

1. Software Licensing and Copyright

ORGANIZATIONS USING cloud services need to be aware of software licensing agreements and copyright laws. Violating licensing agreements or copyright laws can lead to legal consequences.

2. Open Source Software (OSS) Compliance

WHEN USING OPEN SOURCE software in cloud applications, organizations must comply with open source licenses, which can have different requirements for sharing and modifying code.

Conclusion

NAVIGATING THE LEGAL and regulatory landscape in the cloud is complex and ever-changing. Organizations must stay informed about the laws and regulations that apply to their specific industry and geographic location. It's essential to work with legal and compliance experts to develop strategies for cloud adoption that ensure compliance, protect data privacy, and mitigate legal risks. Additionally, cloud service providers often offer compliance resources and tools to assist organizations in meeting their regulatory obligations.

Section 18.3: Data Privacy and Protection in GCP

DATA PRIVACY AND PROTECTION are paramount considerations for organizations utilizing Google Cloud Platform (GCP). GCP provides a robust set of tools and services to help users maintain data privacy, adhere to regulatory requirements, and protect sensitive information. In this section, we will explore key aspects of data privacy and protection within GCP.

Encryption and Data at Rest

GCP EMPLOYS STRONG encryption to safeguard data at rest. When data is stored in GCP services like Cloud Storage, Cloud SQL, or Bigtable, it is automatically encrypted. Google uses the Advanced Encryption Standard (AES) with 256-bit keys to encrypt data at rest. This encryption ensures that even if physical storage devices are compromised, the data remains unreadable without the encryption keys.

Encryption in Transit

DATA TRANSMITTED TO and from GCP services is also encrypted. GCP uses Transport Layer Security (TLS) to encrypt data in transit, ensuring that data remains confidential and secure during transfer. Whether data is moving between a user's location and GCP or between GCP services, it is protected through encryption.

Identity and Access Management (IAM)

GCP'S IDENTITY AND Access Management (IAM) allows organizations to manage access to resources and data. IAM enables administrators to define and control who can access specific resources and what actions they can perform. This granular control helps enforce the principle of least privilege, ensuring that only authorized individuals or services can access sensitive data.

Data Classification and Labeling

DATA CLASSIFICATION and labeling are critical components of data privacy. GCP offers tools like Data Loss Prevention (DLP) to classify and label data based on sensitivity. Organizations can define policies to automatically identify and label sensitive information, such as personally identifiable information (PII) or financial data. This labeling helps in enforcing data access controls and monitoring data movement.

Compliance and Certifications

GCP ADHERES TO VARIOUS industry standards and regulatory certifications, making it suitable for organizations with specific compliance requirements. GCP is certified for standards like ISO 27001, SOC 2, HIPAA, and PCI DSS. These certifications demonstrate GCP's commitment to security and data protection and can assist organizations in meeting their own compliance needs.

Data Access Auditing and Monitoring

GCP PROVIDES COMPREHENSIVE auditing and monitoring capabilities to track data access and changes. Cloud Audit Logs record all user and system activity, including data access and configuration changes. Monitoring tools like Cloud Monitoring and Cloud Logging allow organizations to set up alerts and analyze logs to detect and respond to suspicious activities in real time.

Data Residency and Regional Compliance

GCP OFFERS DATA RESIDENCY options, allowing organizations to specify the geographic location where their data is stored. This feature helps organizations comply with data sovereignty regulations that require data to be stored within specific jurisdictions. Organizations can choose from a wide range of GCP regions to align with their compliance needs.

Conclusion

DATA PRIVACY AND PROTECTION are non-negotiable when working with sensitive information in the cloud. Google Cloud Platform provides a robust set of tools and features to address these concerns effectively. By leveraging encryption, access controls, data classification, compliance certifications, and auditing capabilities, organizations can build secure and compliant solutions on GCP while safeguarding their data and meeting regulatory requirements. It is crucial for organizations to design their GCP environments with data privacy and protection in mind from the outset to ensure a secure and compliant cloud infrastructure.

Section 18.4: Managing Compliance in Multi-Tenant Environments

IN MULTI-TENANT ENVIRONMENTS, multiple organizations or users share the same computing resources and infrastructure, which can introduce unique challenges related to compliance and data security. Google Cloud Platform (GCP) offers several tools and best practices to help organizations manage compliance effectively in such environments.

Isolation and Segmentation

ONE OF THE FUNDAMENTAL aspects of managing compliance in a multi-tenant environment is isolation and segmentation. GCP provides tools like Virtual Private Cloud (VPC) that allow organizations to create isolated networks, subnetworks, and firewall rules. This isolation helps in separating workloads and resources to prevent unauthorized access and data leakage.

Shared Responsibility Model

GCP FOLLOWS A SHARED responsibility model, which means that while Google is responsible for the security of the cloud infrastructure, customers are responsible for securing their data and applications in the cloud. This model emphasizes the importance of customer-side security measures, including access controls, encryption, and compliance configurations.

Identity and Access Management (IAM)

IAM PLAYS A CRUCIAL role in managing access to resources within a multi-tenant environment. Organizations should implement IAM best practices to ensure that users and services have the appropriate permissions and access controls. Role-based access control (RBAC) should be enforced to restrict access to sensitive data and resources.

Data Classification and Labeling

DATA CLASSIFICATION and labeling are essential in multi-tenant environments to identify and protect sensitive data. GCP's Data Loss Prevention (DLP) offers automated data classification and labeling capabilities. Organizations can create policies to classify data based on sensitivity and automatically apply labels. This helps in enforcing access controls and data protection measures.

Auditing and Monitoring

COMPLIANCE IN MULTI-tenant environments requires robust auditing and monitoring. GCP provides tools like Cloud Audit Logs, Cloud Monitoring, and Cloud Logging to track user and system activity. Organizations should configure these tools to monitor for suspicious activities, unauthorized access, and compliance violations. Real-time alerts can be set up to respond promptly to security incidents.

Compliance Frameworks

GCP SUPPORTS VARIOUS compliance frameworks, such as HIPAA, PCI DSS, SOC 2, and more. Organizations in multi-tenant environments can leverage GCP's compliance certifications to demonstrate their adherence to industry-specific regulations. Google undergoes third-party audits and assessments to ensure compliance with these standards, providing confidence to customers.

Security Information and Event Management (SIEM)

IMPLEMENTING A SIEM solution in a multi-tenant environment can enhance security and compliance monitoring. GCP can integrate with SIEM tools to centralize log data and perform advanced threat detection and analysis. This helps organizations detect and respond to security incidents and maintain compliance with regulatory requirements.

Compliance Documentation

MAINTAINING COMPREHENSIVE documentation of security and compliance practices is crucial in multi-tenant environments. Organizations should document their policies, procedures, and configurations related to compliance. This documentation can be used for internal audits, compliance assessments, and demonstrating adherence to regulatory requirements.

Conclusion

MANAGING COMPLIANCE in multi-tenant environments requires a combination of technical controls, best practices, and proactive monitoring. Google Cloud Platform offers a range of tools and features to assist organizations in meeting their compliance objectives. By implementing isolation, access controls, data classification, auditing, and leveraging GCP's compliance certifications, organizations can build secure and compliant solutions in multi-tenant cloud environments while safeguarding data and meeting regulatory standards.

Section 18.5: Case Studies: Compliance and Governance in Action

IN THIS SECTION, WE'LL explore real-world case studies that demonstrate how organizations have successfully implemented compliance and governance practices in the cloud using Google Cloud Platform (GCP). These examples showcase the diverse range of industries and use cases where GCP's tools and features have been instrumental in achieving compliance and governance objectives.

Case Study 1: Healthcare Compliance

INDUSTRY: Healthcare

Challenge: A healthcare organization needed to migrate its sensitive patient data to the cloud while adhering to strict regulatory requirements, including the Health Insurance Portability and Accountability Act (HIPAA).

Solution: The organization chose GCP for its robust security and compliance features. They implemented a secure architecture using GCP's VPC, IAM, and encryption services. They also leveraged GCP's HIPAA compliance offerings, including the HIPAA BAA (Business Associate Agreement). Data was classified, labeled, and access-controlled using GCP's Data Loss Prevention (DLP) and IAM policies. Regular audits and monitoring using Cloud Audit Logs and Cloud Monitoring ensured ongoing compliance.

Outcome: The healthcare organization successfully migrated its data to GCP while maintaining HIPAA compliance. This allowed them to reduce on-premises infrastructure costs, improve scalability, and enhance data security.

Case Study 2: Financial Services Compliance

INDUSTRY: Financial Services

Challenge: A financial institution needed to meet the stringent requirements of the Payment Card Industry Data Security Standard (PCI DSS) while managing its payment processing systems in the cloud.

Solution: The institution selected GCP for its PCI DSS compliance capabilities. They implemented network segmentation using VPCs, applied encryption to data in transit and at rest, and enforced strict access controls using IAM. GCP's compliance certifications, including PCI DSS, reassured the institution. They also integrated a SIEM solution with GCP for real-time monitoring and threat detection.

Outcome: The financial institution achieved and maintained PCI DSS compliance on GCP, ensuring the secure processing of payment card data. They benefited from GCP's scalable infrastructure and enhanced security controls.

Case Study 3: Government Compliance

INDUSTRY: Government

Challenge: A government agency needed to store and manage sensitive citizen data securely in the cloud while adhering to regulatory requirements and data protection laws.

Solution: The agency adopted GCP's government cloud offerings, which include FedRAMP authorization. They implemented strict data access controls, auditing, and encryption. GCP's compliance with government standards reassured the agency. They also used GCP's Cloud Identity and Access Management (Cloud IAM) to manage user permissions effectively. Regular security assessments and audits were conducted to maintain compliance.

Outcome: The government agency securely migrated citizen data to GCP's government cloud, meeting regulatory requirements and ensuring data protection. They achieved cost savings and improved data accessibility.

Case Study 4: Retail Compliance

INDUSTRY: Retail and E-commerce

Challenge: An online retail giant needed to ensure the security of customer payment information and comply with Payment Card

Industry Data Security Standard (PCI DSS) while handling millions of transactions daily.

Solution: The retailer chose GCP for its PCI DSS compliance and data security capabilities. They implemented GCP's secure storage and encryption solutions for payment data. Regular vulnerability scanning and monitoring were carried out using GCP's tools. The retailer also benefited from GCP's global network for fast and reliable service.

Outcome: The retail company achieved and maintained PCI DSS compliance on GCP, ensuring the security of customer payment information. They also experienced improved website performance and scalability during peak shopping seasons.

These case studies highlight how Google Cloud Platform has enabled organizations from various industries to address their compliance and governance needs effectively. By leveraging GCP's security features, compliance certifications, and best practices, these organizations were able to securely and confidently transition to the cloud while meeting their regulatory and industry-specific requirements. These real-world examples demonstrate the versatility and reliability of GCP in supporting compliance and governance initiatives.

Chapter 19: Industry-Specific Solutions with GCP

In this chapter, we will delve into industry-specific solutions and use cases where Google Cloud Platform (GCP) plays a pivotal role in addressing the unique challenges and requirements of various industries. GCP offers a wide array of tools, services, and capabilities that can be tailored to meet the specific needs of sectors such as healthcare, retail, media and entertainment, and financial services. These industry-focused solutions empower organizations to leverage the cloud for innovation, efficiency, and competitive advantage.

Section 19.1: Tailoring GCP for Different Industries

INDUSTRIES TODAY FACE distinct challenges and opportunities, and Google Cloud Platform recognizes the importance of providing tailored solutions. Let's explore how GCP can be customized to suit the needs of different sectors:

1. Healthcare:

HEALTHCARE ORGANIZATIONS handle sensitive patient data and must comply with stringent regulations such as the Health Insurance Portability and Accountability Act (HIPAA). GCP offers healthcare-specific solutions, including HIPAA-compliant services and a Business Associate Agreement (BAA) for covered entities. This enables secure data storage, processing, and sharing in the cloud, while ensuring compliance.

2. Retail and E-commerce:

THE RETAIL INDUSTRY relies on GCP to optimize supply chains, enhance customer experiences, and analyze vast amounts of transactional data. BigQuery, for instance, enables retailers to gain valuable insights from their data, while Cloud Machine Learning aids in personalized recommendations and fraud detection.

3. Media and Entertainment:

MEDIA COMPANIES LEVERAGE GCP for content delivery, media processing, and analytics. Services like Google Cloud CDN, Video AI, and Dataflow enable efficient streaming, content analysis, and real-time audience engagement.

4. Financial Services and Banking:

FINANCIAL INSTITUTIONS trust GCP for secure and compliant cloud services. Encryption, identity and access management, and compliance certifications like PCI DSS are essential for protecting sensitive financial data while meeting regulatory requirements.

5. Manufacturing and Industrial:

MANUFACTURING COMPANIES use GCP's industrial solutions to harness the power of data analytics and machine learning. Predictive maintenance, quality control, and supply chain optimization are areas where GCP contributes to efficiency gains.

6. Education:

EDUCATIONAL INSTITUTIONS benefit from GCP's tools for remote learning, collaboration, and data analysis. G Suite for

Education, Google Classroom, and BigQuery enable effective teaching, learning, and administrative processes.

7. Energy and Utilities:

THE ENERGY SECTOR EMPLOYS GCP for predictive maintenance of infrastructure, optimizing power generation and distribution, and analyzing sensor data from the Internet of Things (IoT) devices. GCP's machine learning and analytics capabilities are crucial in this domain.

8. Telecommunications:

TELECOM COMPANIES USE GCP to develop and deploy 5G applications, analyze network data for optimization, and enhance customer experiences through personalization and recommendation engines.

9. Transportation and Logistics:

GCP ENABLES TRANSPORTATION companies to optimize routes, manage fleets, and improve supply chain visibility. Machine learning and IoT solutions are particularly valuable for predicting maintenance needs and optimizing logistics operations.

10. Government and Public Sector:

GOVERNMENT AGENCIES leverage GCP's secure and compliant cloud services for various applications, including citizen services, data analytics, and disaster response. FedRAMP authorization and data sovereignty options make GCP a reliable choice.

11. Life Sciences and Pharmaceuticals:

THE LIFE SCIENCES INDUSTRY relies on GCP for genomics data analysis, drug discovery, and clinical trials. GCP's scalability and data processing capabilities accelerate research and innovation in this sector.

In each of these industries, GCP provides a foundation for digital transformation, innovation, and addressing unique challenges. The flexibility and scalability of GCP's infrastructure and services allow organizations to tailor their solutions to specific industry needs, fostering growth and competitiveness. Throughout this chapter, we will explore real-world examples and case studies that showcase how organizations within these industries have successfully harnessed GCP's capabilities to drive innovation and achieve their goals.

Section 19.2: Healthcare and Life Sciences on GCP

THE HEALTHCARE AND life sciences industry is one of the most regulated and data-intensive sectors globally. With Google Cloud Platform (GCP), organizations within this industry can harness the power of cloud computing to streamline operations, accelerate research, and improve patient care while ensuring compliance with strict regulatory standards.

1. Data Security and Compliance:

ONE OF THE PRIMARY concerns in healthcare is the security of patient data and compliance with regulations like HIPAA (Health Insurance Portability and Accountability Act). GCP offers healthcare-specific solutions designed to meet these requirements. Organizations can utilize encryption, access controls, and audit logging to safeguard sensitive patient information.

2. Research and Genomics:

GCP PROVIDES A ROBUST infrastructure for genomics research and analysis. Researchers can leverage tools like Google Genomics and BigQuery to process and analyze vast datasets of genomic information quickly. This enables discoveries related to disease genetics, personalized medicine, and drug development.

3. Telemedicine and Remote Patient Monitoring:

THE ADVENT OF TELEMEDICINE has been accelerated by GCP's capabilities. Healthcare providers can build telehealth applications that facilitate remote consultations, diagnostics, and monitoring. This is especially crucial in ensuring access to healthcare services, even in remote areas.

4. Healthcare Analytics:

BIG DATA ANALYTICS is transforming healthcare by providing insights into patient outcomes, treatment effectiveness, and population health trends. GCP's data analytics tools, including BigQuery and Data Studio, empower healthcare organizations to derive actionable insights from their data, leading to better decision-making.

5. Imaging and Diagnostics:

MEDICAL IMAGING, SUCH as MRI and CT scans, generates vast amounts of data. GCP's storage and processing capabilities enable healthcare providers to store and analyze these images efficiently. Machine learning models can assist in image interpretation, aiding radiologists and improving diagnostic accuracy.

6. Drug Discovery and Clinical Trials:

PHARMACEUTICAL COMPANIES and research organizations leverage GCP to accelerate drug discovery and streamline clinical trials. Cloud-based computing resources and machine learning algorithms expedite the identification of potential drug candidates and the analysis of trial data.

7. Electronic Health Records (EHR) and Interoperability:

GCP SUPPORTS THE STORAGE and sharing of electronic health records (EHR) while ensuring data interoperability. Healthcare systems can use APIs and standards to exchange patient information securely and efficiently.

8. Disaster Recovery and Business Continuity:

HEALTHCARE ORGANIZATIONS require robust disaster recovery and business continuity plans to ensure uninterrupted patient care. GCP's cloud infrastructure offers solutions for data backup, failover, and disaster recovery, reducing downtime and data loss risks.

9. Collaborative Research:

GCP FOSTERS COLLABORATION among healthcare institutions and researchers. Shared datasets, secure access controls, and collaboration tools like Google Workspace facilitate collaborative research projects, leading to breakthroughs in medical science.

10. Patient Engagement and Experience:

BY LEVERAGING GCP'S AI and machine learning capabilities, healthcare providers can enhance patient engagement through personalized recommendations, chatbots, and virtual assistants. These technologies improve patient experiences and streamline administrative processes.

In summary, Google Cloud Platform empowers the healthcare and life sciences industry to advance patient care, drive medical research, and comply with regulatory standards. Its scalable infrastructure, data analytics tools, and security features make it an invaluable resource for organizations committed to improving health outcomes and revolutionizing the healthcare landscape. Throughout this section, we will explore specific use cases and success stories within the healthcare and life sciences domain, highlighting the transformative impact of GCP.

Section 19.3: GCP in Retail and E-commerce

THE RETAIL AND E-COMMERCE industry is undergoing a significant digital transformation, driven by changing consumer preferences and the need for seamless online shopping experiences. Google Cloud Platform (GCP) offers a wide range of services and solutions to help retailers and e-commerce businesses adapt to these changes, improve operations, and provide exceptional customer experiences.

1. Personalized Shopping Experiences:

GCP ENABLES RETAILERS to leverage customer data to create personalized shopping experiences. By analyzing customer behavior and preferences, retailers can offer tailored product recommendations, pricing, and promotions, increasing customer satisfaction and conversion rates.

2. Inventory Management and Supply Chain Optimization:

EFFICIENT INVENTORY management and supply chain operations are critical in the retail industry. GCP's data analytics tools can provide insights into demand forecasting, inventory optimization, and supply chain efficiency, reducing costs and ensuring products are available when customers need them.

3. E-commerce Platforms and Mobile Apps:

RETAILERS CAN BUILD and host their e-commerce websites and mobile apps on GCP, benefiting from its scalable and reliable infrastructure. Google Kubernetes Engine (GKE) allows for the deployment of containerized applications, ensuring high availability during peak shopping seasons.

4. Fraud Detection and Prevention:

E-COMMERCE BUSINESSES often face challenges related to fraud and security. GCP offers advanced machine learning and AI capabilities to detect and prevent fraudulent transactions in real-time, safeguarding both customers and the business.

5. Customer Analytics and Insights:

UNDERSTANDING CUSTOMER behavior is crucial for retailers. GCP's data analytics and machine learning tools help retailers gain insights into customer preferences, shopping patterns, and lifetime value, enabling data-driven decisions and marketing strategies.

6. Omnichannel Retailing:

GCP SUPPORTS OMNICHANNEL retailing by providing a unified platform for managing online and offline sales channels. Retailers can offer seamless shopping experiences, allowing customers to shop via multiple channels and access consistent product information and pricing.

7. Point of Sale (POS) Solutions:

GCP CAN BE USED TO develop and deploy cloud-based POS systems that enhance the checkout experience. These solutions offer flexibility, scalability, and real-time reporting, making it easier for retailers to manage their stores efficiently.

8. Customer Support and Chatbots:

RETAILERS CAN IMPLEMENT AI-powered chatbots and virtual assistants on their websites and mobile apps. These chatbots can handle customer inquiries, provide product information, and assist with the shopping process, enhancing customer support and reducing response times.

9. Recommendations and Personalization:

GCP'S AI AND MACHINE learning capabilities can be used to create recommendation engines that suggest products based on customer preferences and browsing history. This increases cross-selling and upselling opportunities.

10. Scalability and Global Reach:

GCP'S GLOBAL NETWORK of data centers ensures that e-commerce websites and applications can scale to meet the demands of customers worldwide. Retailers can expand their reach and handle traffic spikes during promotions and sales events.

In conclusion, Google Cloud Platform offers a comprehensive suite of services and solutions tailored to the needs of the retail and e-commerce industry. Retailers and e-commerce businesses can leverage GCP's capabilities to improve customer experiences, optimize operations, and stay competitive in the rapidly evolving digital landscape. Throughout this section, we will explore specific use cases and success stories within the retail and e-commerce sector, showcasing how GCP is driving innovation and growth in this industry.

Section 19.4: Media and Entertainment Solutions

THE MEDIA AND ENTERTAINMENT industry has experienced a digital revolution in recent years, with streaming services, online content creation, and personalized experiences becoming the norm. Google Cloud Platform (GCP) offers a wide array of services and solutions tailored to the unique needs of this industry, helping media companies, broadcasters, and content creators deliver engaging content to their audiences and optimize their operations.

1. Content Delivery and Streaming:

GCP PROVIDES A ROBUST content delivery network (CDN) that ensures low-latency content delivery to viewers worldwide. Media companies can use Google Cloud CDN to distribute video, audio, and other media content efficiently, reducing buffering and improving user experiences.

2. Media Processing and Transcoding:

MEDIA CONTENT OFTEN needs to be transcoded into various formats for different devices and bandwidths. GCP offers Media Transcoding, a scalable and cost-effective solution that automates the process of converting media files into multiple formats, ensuring compatibility and high-quality playback.

3. Content Recommendation and Personalization:

PERSONALIZED CONTENT recommendations are essential for keeping viewers engaged. GCP's machine learning capabilities enable media companies to analyze user behavior, preferences, and viewing history to deliver tailored content recommendations, increasing viewer satisfaction and retention.

4. Analytics and Viewer Insights:

UNDERSTANDING VIEWER behavior and preferences is crucial for content creators and broadcasters. GCP's data analytics tools can process vast amounts of viewer data, providing actionable insights into content performance, audience demographics, and advertising effectiveness.

5. Cloud-Based Editing and Collaboration:

CONTENT CREATORS CAN take advantage of GCP's cloud-based video editing tools to streamline the content creation process. Collaborative editing, real-time feedback, and version control simplify the production workflow, allowing teams to work efficiently, whether they are in the same location or distributed globally.

6. Live Streaming and Event Coverage:

GCP OFFERS SOLUTIONS for live streaming events, such as sports, concerts, and conferences. Media companies can leverage Google Cloud's global infrastructure to deliver high-quality live streams with low latency to a global audience.

7. Archiving and Digital Asset Management:

MANAGING AND PRESERVING media assets is essential for media organizations. GCP's cloud storage solutions and digital asset management tools provide a secure and scalable way to store, catalog, and retrieve media assets, ensuring accessibility and compliance.

8. Monetization and Advertising:

MEDIA COMPANIES CAN monetize their content through various advertising models. GCP's ad-serving solutions enable targeted advertising, ad insertion, and real-time bidding, maximizing revenue while delivering relevant ads to viewers.

9. Content Security and DRM:

PROTECTING INTELLECTUAL property and content rights is paramount in the media industry. GCP offers Digital Rights Management (DRM) solutions to secure content distribution and prevent unauthorized access or piracy.

10. Interactive Experiences and Augmented Reality (AR):

WITH GCP'S AR AND INTERACTIVE media capabilities, content creators can develop immersive experiences that engage viewers in new ways. Augmented reality overlays, interactive videos, and gamified content enhance viewer engagement and interactivity.

In summary, Google Cloud Platform empowers media and entertainment companies to stay competitive and innovative in a rapidly evolving landscape. Whether it's delivering high-quality content, understanding audience behavior, or monetizing through advertising, GCP provides the tools and infrastructure needed to excel in the digital media and entertainment industry. Throughout this section, we will explore real-world examples and use cases that illustrate how GCP is transforming the media and entertainment landscape.

Section 19.5: GCP for Financial Services and Banking

THE FINANCIAL SERVICES and banking sector is one of the most heavily regulated and data-intensive industries, and it demands secure, scalable, and innovative solutions. Google Cloud Platform (GCP) offers a range of services tailored to meet the unique needs and challenges faced by financial institutions, from traditional banks to fintech startups. In this section, we will explore how GCP is transforming the financial services landscape.

1. Data Security and Compliance:

SECURITY AND COMPLIANCE are paramount in the financial sector. GCP provides robust security features, including encryption, identity and access management (IAM), and audit logging. GCP's compliance certifications, including SOC 2, PCI DSS, and ISO 27001, help financial institutions meet regulatory requirements.

2. Data Analytics and Insights:

FINANCIAL ORGANIZATIONS generate vast amounts of data. GCP's data analytics tools, such as BigQuery and Dataflow, enable real-time data analysis, fraud detection, and risk assessment. Machine learning models can identify patterns and anomalies in financial data, improving decision-making.

3. Customer Experience and Personalization:

ENHANCING THE CUSTOMER experience is a priority for financial institutions. GCP's machine learning and AI capabilities can analyze customer data to provide personalized product recommendations, improve customer service through chatbots, and streamline onboarding processes.

4. Core Banking and Payment Processing:

GCP OFFERS SOLUTIONS for core banking systems and payment processing. Financial organizations can leverage Google Cloud's infrastructure for high availability and scalability, ensuring uninterrupted services for customers.

5. Regulatory Reporting and Compliance:

MEETING REGULATORY reporting requirements is a complex task. GCP's data storage and processing capabilities facilitate the collection, storage, and analysis of data needed for regulatory compliance, simplifying reporting processes.

6. Fraud Detection and Prevention:

DETECTING AND PREVENTING fraud is crucial in the financial industry. GCP's machine learning models can analyze transaction data in real-time, identifying suspicious activities and helping institutions take immediate action to mitigate risks.

7. Trading and Investment:

GCP PROVIDES THE INFRASTRUCTURE and data analytics tools necessary for algorithmic trading, portfolio management, and risk assessment. Financial organizations can leverage GCP's low-latency network and data processing capabilities for real-time trading decisions.

8. Asset Management and Wealthtech:

ASSET MANAGEMENT FIRMS and wealthtech startups can benefit from GCP's data analytics and machine learning capabilities to optimize investment strategies, create custom investment products, and enhance client experiences.

9. Blockchain and Distributed Ledger Technology (DLT):

GCP OFFERS SOLUTIONS for blockchain and DLT applications. Financial organizations can explore use cases such as supply chain finance, digital identity, and cross-border payments using GCP's blockchain offerings.

10. Cloud Cost Management:

FINANCIAL INSTITUTIONS can optimize their cloud costs using GCP's cost management tools. Cost allocation, budgeting, and resource optimization features help control cloud expenditure while maintaining scalability and performance.

In conclusion, GCP is a strategic partner for financial services and banking institutions looking to innovate, improve security, and enhance customer experiences. The cloud platform's advanced capabilities in data analytics, machine learning, and compliance management enable financial organizations to navigate a rapidly changing industry landscape while ensuring data security and regulatory compliance. This section will delve into specific use cases and success stories from the financial services sector that demonstrate the transformative power of GCP.

Chapter 20: The Future of GCP and Cloud Computing

Section 20.1: Emerging Trends in Cloud Computing

THE CLOUD COMPUTING landscape is ever-evolving, driven by technological advancements, changing business needs, and emerging trends. As we look ahead to the future of Google Cloud Platform (GCP) and cloud computing in general, it's essential to stay informed about the latest trends that will shape the industry. In this section, we'll explore some of the emerging trends in cloud computing that will likely influence the direction of GCP and cloud services in the coming years.

1. Edge Computing and IoT Integration:

AS MORE IOT (INTERNET of Things) devices are deployed worldwide, there's a growing need for edge computing solutions. Edge computing allows data processing to occur closer to the data source, reducing latency and improving real-time decision-making. GCP is poised to expand its edge computing capabilities, enabling organizations to leverage the power of IoT and edge devices seamlessly.

2. Serverless Computing and Microservices:

SERVERLESS COMPUTING has gained significant traction due to its scalability and cost-effectiveness. GCP's serverless offerings, such as Cloud Functions and App Engine, are likely to evolve further, making it easier for developers to build and deploy microservices-based applications.

3. AI and Machine Learning Integration:

AI AND MACHINE LEARNING will continue to be at the forefront of cloud innovation. GCP's AI Platform and AutoML services will become even more advanced, allowing organizations to leverage AI-driven insights and automation in various domains.

4. Multi-Cloud and Hybrid Cloud Adoption:

MANY ORGANIZATIONS are adopting multi-cloud and hybrid cloud strategies to avoid vendor lock-in and increase flexibility. GCP's Anthos platform and hybrid cloud solutions will play a crucial role in this trend, enabling seamless management of resources across different cloud environments.

5. Quantum Computing Advancements:

QUANTUM COMPUTING IS still in its early stages, but it holds immense potential for solving complex problems. Google has been actively researching quantum computing, and GCP is likely to incorporate quantum computing services as they mature.

6. Enhanced Security and Privacy:

WITH THE INCREASING importance of data privacy and security regulations, cloud providers like GCP will continue to enhance their security features. Expect more robust encryption, identity management, and compliance tools.

7. Cloud-Native Development and DevOps:

CLOUD-NATIVE DEVELOPMENT practices and DevOps methodologies will continue to gain prominence. GCP's tools for container orchestration (e.g., Kubernetes) and CI/CD (e.g., Cloud Build) will remain vital for organizations adopting these practices.

8. Environmental Sustainability:

SUSTAINABILITY IS BECOMING a priority in the cloud industry. GCP has committed to being carbon-neutral since 2007 and aims to operate on 24/7 carbon-free energy by 2030. Expect more sustainability initiatives and options for environmentally conscious organizations.

9. 5G Integration:

THE ROLLOUT OF 5G NETWORKS will enable faster and more reliable connections, opening up new possibilities for cloud applications. GCP will continue to explore opportunities for 5G integration and low-latency services.

10. Blockchain and Decentralized Applications (DApps):

BLOCKCHAIN TECHNOLOGY is being used beyond cryptocurrencies, and GCP may offer more services for blockchain development and decentralized applications in the future.

In conclusion, the future of GCP and cloud computing is filled with exciting possibilities. Staying informed about these emerging trends and understanding how GCP can adapt and innovate will be essential for organizations looking to harness the full potential of cloud technology in the years to come. This section will provide insights into how GCP is positioning itself to address these trends and drive innovation in cloud computing.

Section 20.2: Innovations in GCP: What's Next?

GOOGLE CLOUD PLATFORM (GCP) has a history of continuous innovation, and its commitment to staying at the forefront of cloud technology is unwavering. In this section, we'll delve into some of the innovations and advancements we can expect from GCP in the near future.

1. Advanced AI and Machine Learning Services:

GCP'S AI AND MACHINE learning services are poised for significant advancements. Expect more pre-built models, improved natural language understanding, and advanced computer vision capabilities. GCP will continue to democratize AI, making it accessible to a broader range of users.

2. Enhanced Data Analytics:

DATA ANALYTICS WILL become more powerful and user-friendly on GCP. Real-time analytics, predictive analytics, and advanced data visualization tools will be part of GCP's arsenal. Look out for improvements in services like BigQuery and Data Studio.

3. AI-Driven Automation:

GCP WILL INCORPORATE AI-driven automation across its services. This includes automated resource scaling, intelligent anomaly detection, and predictive maintenance. Organizations can expect to reduce operational overhead while improving system reliability.

4. Hybrid and Multi-Cloud Innovations:

THE HYBRID AND MULTI-cloud capabilities of GCP will evolve further. Anthos will become even more versatile, enabling seamless application management across on-premises and multiple cloud providers. Expect enhanced security and compliance features in this context.

5. Serverless and Event-Driven Architectures:

SERVERLESS COMPUTING will continue to gain prominence. GCP's serverless offerings, like Cloud Functions and Eventarc, will become more feature-rich and easier to use. Developers can build event-driven architectures with greater ease.

6. Quantum Computing Integration:

QUANTUM COMPUTING IS an area where Google has been investing heavily. While quantum computing is still in its early stages, GCP may offer early access to quantum computing resources and services, allowing organizations to explore quantum solutions.

7. Enhanced Security Posture:

SECURITY WILL REMAIN a top priority for GCP. Expect continuous improvements in identity and access management, threat detection, and encryption services. Zero-trust security models will become more accessible to organizations of all sizes.

8. Sustainability Initiatives:

GOOGLE'S COMMITMENT to sustainability will reflect in GCP's offerings. Look for more data center locations powered by renewable energy, carbon-neutral cloud services, and tools to help organizations reduce their carbon footprint.

9. Edge Computing Solutions:

EDGE COMPUTING WILL play a more significant role in GCP's ecosystem. Expect specialized edge services and tools for developing and managing edge applications. GCP will facilitate the deployment of applications closer to the data source.

10. Community and Collaboration:

GCP WILL FOSTER A VIBRANT community and collaboration ecosystem. More developer resources, community-driven initiatives, and collaborative tools will be introduced to empower GCP users and foster innovation.

In conclusion, GCP's future is bright and filled with innovation. Organizations that choose to build their infrastructure and applications on GCP can anticipate a rich set of cutting-edge services and tools to support their digital transformation journey. This section has provided a glimpse into some of the innovations that are on the horizon for GCP, and it's an exciting time for cloud technology enthusiasts and organizations alike.

Section 20.3: The Role of AI and Machine Learning in Future Cloud Solutions

ARTIFICIAL INTELLIGENCE (AI) and Machine Learning (ML) have emerged as transformative technologies in the world of cloud computing. In this section, we will explore the pivotal role that AI and ML are set to play in shaping the future of cloud solutions, including their integration with Google Cloud Platform (GCP).

1. AI-Driven Automation:

AI AND ML ARE AT THE heart of automation in cloud computing. They enable intelligent decision-making, predictive analytics, and automation of routine tasks. In the future, AI-driven automation will further enhance the efficiency and reliability of cloud services. Tasks like resource scaling, security monitoring, and performance optimization will be automated to a greater extent.

2. Enhanced Data Insights:

AI AND ML ALGORITHMS are becoming more adept at extracting valuable insights from vast amounts of data. In the cloud, this translates to improved data analytics and business intelligence. GCP's BigQuery and Dataflow services, combined with AI, will provide organizations with deeper and more actionable insights from their data.

3. Personalized User Experiences:

AI-POWERED RECOMMENDATION engines and personalization will be integrated into cloud applications. Whether it's content recommendations in media streaming or product suggestions in e-commerce, AI will make user experiences more tailored and engaging.

4. Advanced Security and Threat Detection:

AI AND ML ARE INDISPENSABLE in the fight against cyber threats. Future cloud solutions will leverage AI to detect and respond to security incidents in real-time. GCP's Cloud Security Command Center and AI-driven anomaly detection will play a crucial role in this regard.

5. Natural Language Understanding:

CONVERSATIONAL AI AND natural language understanding will become standard features in cloud applications. Chatbots and virtual assistants will provide human-like interactions, making customer support and user interactions more efficient.

6. AutoML and Democratization of AI:

GOOGLE'S AUTOML INITIATIVES will continue to make AI more accessible to non-experts. Organizations will be able to build custom machine learning models with ease, opening up new possibilities for industry-specific solutions.

7. Real-Time Decision-Making:

EDGE COMPUTING AND AI will enable real-time decision-making at the edge. This is especially critical for applications where low latency is crucial, such as autonomous vehicles, industrial automation, and augmented reality.

8. AI Ethics and Governance:

WITH THE INCREASING adoption of AI, ethical considerations and governance will become paramount. Cloud providers like GCP will offer tools and frameworks to ensure responsible AI development and deployment, addressing concerns related to bias, fairness, and transparency.

9. Quantum Machine Learning:

AS QUANTUM COMPUTING advances, it will intersect with machine learning. Future cloud solutions may offer quantum machine learning capabilities, allowing organizations to solve complex problems that are currently infeasible with classical computing.

10. Continuous Innovation:

AI AND ML ARE DYNAMIC fields, and cloud providers like GCP are committed to continuous innovation. Expect regular updates and enhancements to AI and ML services, keeping them at the cutting edge of technology.

In conclusion, AI and ML are poised to drive innovation and transformation in future cloud solutions. GCP's integration of AI and ML capabilities will empower organizations to harness the full potential of these technologies, enabling them to stay competitive and deliver enhanced services to their customers. The role of AI and ML in the cloud is not just about automation; it's about unlocking new possibilities and shaping the future of computing.

Section 20.4: Preparing for the Next Wave of Cloud Computing

THE FUTURE OF CLOUD computing promises exciting advancements and challenges. To prepare for the next wave of cloud innovation, businesses and IT professionals need to consider several key factors.

1. Edge Computing Expansion:

EDGE COMPUTING WILL continue to gain prominence. Organizations should evaluate how they can leverage edge resources to reduce latency, enhance real-time decision-making, and improve the user experience. Edge-compatible cloud solutions, like Google's Anthos, will be essential for managing distributed environments effectively.

2. Hybrid and Multi-Cloud Adoption:

AS HYBRID AND MULTI-cloud strategies become more prevalent, organizations need to focus on seamless integration between on-premises, public cloud, and multi-cloud environments. Cloud management platforms like Google Cloud's Anthos will simplify the orchestration and management of resources across different cloud providers and data centers.

3. Containerization and Kubernetes:

CONTAINERIZATION AND Kubernetes are fundamental to modern cloud-native applications. Businesses should invest in container orchestration skills and explore how to optimize their applications for container deployment. Kubernetes will remain a critical technology for managing and scaling containers in the cloud.

4. Serverless Computing:

SERVERLESS COMPUTING will continue to evolve, offering cost-effective, event-driven solutions. Organizations should identify use cases where serverless architectures can improve efficiency and reduce operational overhead. Google Cloud Functions and App Engine are notable offerings in this space.

5. AI and ML Integration:

AI AND ML WILL PERMEATE all aspects of cloud computing. Businesses should prepare for AI-driven automation, enhanced data analytics, and AI-powered security. Upskilling employees in AI and ML will be crucial for staying competitive.

6. Quantum Computing Readiness:

WHILE QUANTUM COMPUTING is still in its infancy, it's wise to monitor developments in this field. Businesses should stay informed about potential quantum computing applications and how they might impact their industry.

7. Security and Compliance Focus:

WITH THE GROWING COMPLEXITY of cloud ecosystems, security and compliance will remain paramount. Organizations should implement robust security practices, including encryption, identity and access management, and compliance auditing. Cloud providers like Google Cloud offer extensive security tools and services.

8. Cost Optimization Strategies:

CLOUD COSTS CAN ESCALATE if not managed effectively. Businesses should continue to optimize their cloud spending by monitoring resource usage, leveraging cost management tools, and exploring reserved instances or committed use contracts.

9. Resilience and Disaster Recovery:

UNFORESEEN DISRUPTIONS can occur, so disaster recovery planning is essential. Organizations should assess their disaster recovery strategies, including data backup, replication, and business continuity plans. Google Cloud provides tools for building resilient architectures.

10. Continuous Learning and Adaptation:

CLOUD TECHNOLOGY EVOLVES rapidly. IT professionals and organizations should commit to continuous learning, staying updated with the latest cloud trends, and adapting their strategies accordingly. Certification programs and training resources from cloud providers can be valuable for skill development.

In summary, the future of cloud computing holds tremendous potential for innovation and growth. Embracing edge computing, hybrid and multi-cloud strategies, containerization, serverless computing, AI and ML, and staying prepared for emerging technologies like quantum computing are vital steps for organizations to thrive in the evolving cloud landscape. Moreover, maintaining a strong focus on security, cost optimization, resilience, and continuous learning will be essential for success.

Section 20.5: Conclusion: Embracing the Cloud Future with GCP

AS WE CONCLUDE OUR journey through the vast landscape of Google Cloud Platform (GCP) and cloud computing, it's essential to reflect on the transformative power of the cloud and the role GCP plays in shaping the future of technology and business. This section serves as a final note, summarizing key takeaways and encouraging organizations and individuals to embrace the cloud future with GCP.

1. Cloud Computing's Impact:

CLOUD COMPUTING HAS revolutionized the way organizations operate, enabling agility, scalability, and innovation. It has paved the way for digital transformation, allowing businesses to adapt to changing landscapes quickly.

2. GCP's Contribution:

GOOGLE CLOUD PLATFORM has emerged as a leading cloud provider, offering a comprehensive suite of services, cutting-edge technologies, and a global network of data centers. From infrastructure and data analytics to machine learning and IoT, GCP empowers businesses to harness the full potential of the cloud.

3. Continuous Learning:

THE CLOUD LANDSCAPE is dynamic, with new features and services continually being introduced. To stay competitive, individuals and organizations must commit to lifelong learning. Google Cloud provides extensive training resources, certification programs, and a supportive community.

4. Innovation and Transformation:

GCP FOSTERS INNOVATION by providing tools and platforms for creating next-generation applications, leveraging AI and ML, and driving data-driven insights. It enables businesses to transform and disrupt industries.

5. Security and Compliance:

GOOGLE CLOUD PLACES a strong emphasis on security, compliance, and data protection. Organizations can trust GCP to provide robust security tools, identity management, encryption, and compliance certifications.

6. Collaboration and Community:

GCP'S COLLABORATIVE ecosystem encourages developers, data scientists, and IT professionals to work together, share knowledge, and build innovative solutions. The Google Cloud community is vibrant, with forums, events, and partnerships.

7. Cost Efficiency:

COST MANAGEMENT IS critical in the cloud. GCP offers cost optimization tools and flexible pricing options to help organizations control expenses while benefiting from cloud capabilities.

8. Global Reach:

GCP'S EXTENSIVE GLOBAL network and data center presence enable businesses to expand globally with ease. The platform's low-latency, high-performance infrastructure supports applications worldwide.

9. The Future Awaits:

THE CLOUD'S EVOLUTION is far from over. Emerging technologies like edge computing, quantum computing, and advanced AI will continue to shape the future. GCP is positioned to lead in these areas.

10. Embrace the Cloud Future:

IN CONCLUSION, THE cloud is not just a technology; it's a mindset and a catalyst for innovation. Embrace the cloud future with GCP by exploring its vast ecosystem, staying curious, and leveraging its capabilities to drive your organization's success.

The journey through this book has been a comprehensive exploration of Google Cloud Platform, its services, best practices, and real-world applications. We hope it has equipped you with the knowledge and inspiration needed to embark on your cloud journey confidently. As you navigate the ever-changing technology landscape, remember that the cloud offers limitless possibilities, and GCP is your trusted partner in harnessing them.

www.ingramcontent.com/pod-product-compliance
Lightning Source LLC
LaVergne TN
LVHW090305210926
848480LV00001B/133